THE ILLUSTRATED
DICTIONARY
OF
PHOTOGRAPHY

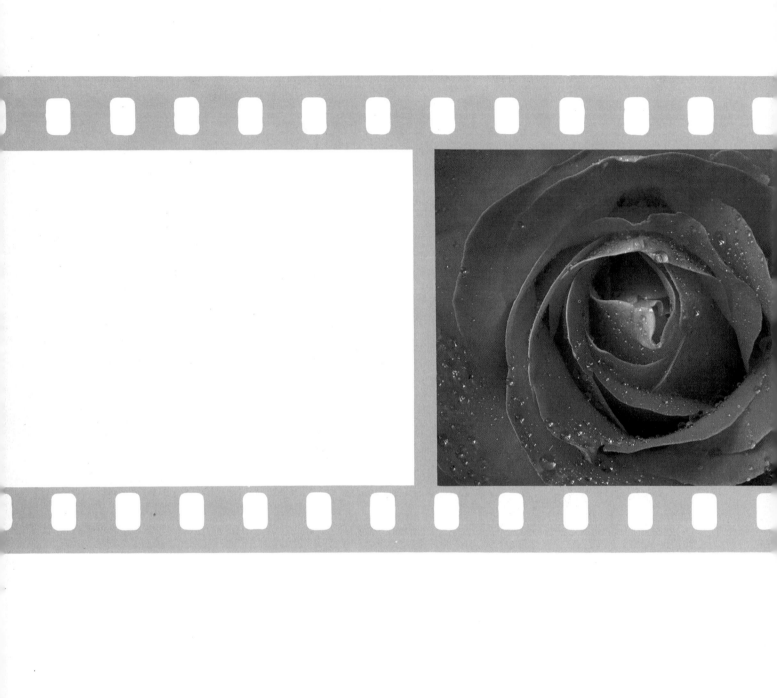

THE ILLUSTRATED
DICTIONARY
OF
PHOTOGRAPHY

Adrian Bailey

WINDWARD

Executive Managers Kelly Flynn
Susan Egerton-Jones
Art Editor Hans Verkroost
Consultant Editor Richard Platt
Editorial Assistant Stephen Bowden
Production Peter Phillips

This edition published 1987 by WINDWARD
an imprint owned by W.H. Smith & Son Limited
Registered No 237811 England Trading as WHS Distributors
St John's House, East Street, Leicester LE1 6NE

Edited and designed by the Artists House
Division of Mitchell Beazley International Ltd.
Artists House
14–15 Manette Street
London W1V 5LB

An Artists House Book
© Mitchell Beazley Publishers 1987

ISBN 0 7112 0479 9

Typeset by Hourds Typographica, Stafford.
Reproduced by La Cromolito s.n.c., Milan.
Printed in Portugal by Printer Portuguesa Grafica Lda.

INTRODUCTION

If this book were to be totally comprehensive, it would run into many volumes and take years to complete. I wanted to write a book for the here and now rather than the future – a book that I would use myself when I had remembered the principle but had forgotten the detail.

It is, I believe, rather more than a reference dictionary being both practical and historically informative – a book for all photographers, amateur or professional, who would reach for the bookshelf to refresh their memories on a technical detail or an intriguing fact: how autofocus works; Fox Talbot's litigious nature; how to take a pinhole picture with a jam pot cover; Scott Archer's modest but inventive genius; Muybridge's eccentricity (and violent character); how to exploit depth of field; Edwin Land's daughter's demand for an "instant picture" that founded the Polaroid Corporation; Hurter and Driffield's quest for a standard means of exposure; how to exploit depth of field; who invented the Petzval lens (it was Joseph Petzval in 1840 – he saw the need for a "fast" lens for portraiture to avoid the lengthy exposures that forced sitters into unnatural rigidity).

I have tried to distil all the information to obtain the essence of fact. Having always been fascinated by the history of photography as much as by technological progress, I am inclined to wander down the odd photographic byway, but my learned friend and technical editor Richard Platt has ensured that I did not forget such essential entries as "camera" and "photography", and the book's designer, Hans Verkroost, has enhanced plain fact and statistic with attractive and informative pictures.

Alongside the standard and important technical references are entries on the famous as well as the unsung heroes of photographic history – the innovators who advanced, often at great odds and sometimes against each other, the cause and course of photography. But I have not included photographers – those practitioners who took the camera and established an enduring, universally popular means of recording and communicating. You will not find Ansel Adams, Steichen, Brassai, Bert Hardy, Cartier-Bresson or Margaret Bourke White here, but I hope you will find a great deal else to fascinate and enlighten.

Adrian Bailey

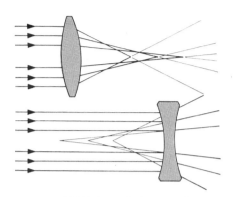

ABERRATION: Lens designers reduce aberration by combining converging (A) and diverging (B) lenses.

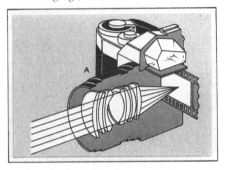

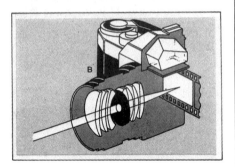

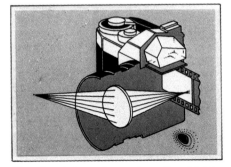

Stopping down reduces aberration. Light patches (coma) are formed by oblique rays.

Aberration

Inherent optical defect in a lens causing unsharp or distorted images. No lens is perfect, and the correction of aberrations is one of the most important elements of lens design. It is achieved principally by combining single lenses in such a way that the aberrations in one lens are corrected by opposing aberrations in another. While it is relatively easy to correct any particular aberration in this way, it is much harder to achieve an overall balance, as compensation for one error can increase another. To this extent all lens design is an exercise in compromise. There are two main types of aberration: spherical, or focus distorting; and chromatic, or colour distorting. Both are caused by the fact that light rays passing through a simple lens do not focus upon a common point. Rays passing through the outer part of a lens are subject to greater refraction than those passing through the central zone and thus in the case of a convex lens come to focus nearer the lens. Similarly, the different colours of the SPECTRUM which make up white light are subject to different degrees of REFRACTION so that blue light rays passing through a lens reach a point of focus nearer to the lens than the green and red rays. Lenses corrected by the use of different types of glass to bring two colours to a common focus are known as achromatic; most modern lenses are of this type. Those corrected for blue, green and red WAVELENGTHS are called apochromatic; they are very expensive to produce and used mainly in technical work. The effects of both spherical and chromatic aberration are minimized by using a small APERTURE, since then the light passes through only the central part of the lens where curvature and hence differences in refraction are at their least. Both types of distortion affect images formed by light passing through the lens from

any angle, including along the lens's AXIS, but there are five other principal types of aberration that are caused only by off-axis images, and are thus most pronounced with wide-angle lenses. These are: (1) Lateral chromatic aberration, which causes images to vary in size according to their colour. The more oblique the image, the greater the distortion caused by the spreading of the different wavelengths. This aberration cannot be corrected by stopping down, which affects depth of field rather than magnification. (2) Coma, an exaggerated form of spherical aberration in which an off-axis point is imaged as a series of tiny overlapping circles forming a tailed shape like a comet – hence the name. (3) Astigmatism, produced when a lens is unable to simultaneously focus lines at right angles to each other near the edge of the field, giving a compromise image with blurred edges. (4) Curvature of field, which is the failure of a lens to convey an overall sharp image in a flat plane – the film. Images of distant objects are formed closer to the lens than those of near objects, and when a flat surface parallel to the FOCAL PLANE is imaged, the top, bottom and edges of that surface are further away from the lens than the central part. In a lens uncorrected for field curvature, it might not be possible to focus the edges and centre of the surface at the same time. (5) Distortion, which occurs when off-axis rays of light passing through parts of the lens other than the centre are spread so that the magnification of the image varies across the focal plane. Thus shape, not sharpness, is affected. Where the edges of the image bow outwards, the effect is known as barrel distortion; where they bow inwards, the term pincushion distortion is used. Coma, astigmatism and field curvature are all reduced by stopping down, but not distortion, which varies with the position of the aperture relative to the lens. The best modern lenses are of such high quality that their user will seldom be concerned with aberration problems, although ZOOM LENSES rarely match the performance of their fixed-focal equivalents. Orthodox lenses can cope with most situations, and more specialist lenses take care of others. Lenses for aerial photography, for example, are made to give optimum flatness of field and sharp definition over the entire picture area when focused at infinity and operating at high shutter speeds (because of the motion of the aircraft) and consequently wide aperture. They are also chromatically corrected to compensate for the yellow, orange or red filters normally used with them. As well as providing problems to be overcome by the technician, aberration can also be exploited creatively. Soft focus lenses, deliberately under-compensated for spherical aberration, are, for example, favourite tools of the portrait photographer.

Abrasion marks

Scratches and abrasions on processed photographic emulsion. They can be caused in a number of ways, most usually during loading or processing. Abrasion marks are difficult to remove, but less severe examples can be erased by rubbing the mark with cotton wool and methylated spirit, or can be prevented from appearing on an enlarged print by using diffuse illumination when enlarging.

Absorption

Taking up of light energy by matter and its transformation into heat. Light-waves are either absorbed or reflected by the surfaces upon which they fall, colour being the result of selective absorption. Black absorbs most of the SPECTRUM, whereas white surfaces reflect all the colours, combining to give white light;

similarly, a red surface absorbs blue and green light, reflecting red. Absorption can be calculated by measuring the absorbed part of a light-wave against colour. Plotting such figures on a graph produces an 'absorption curve', which is a very valuable aid in determining certain characteristics of colour materials and filters.

Accelerator

A chemical, invariably an alkali, added to the developer to increase rate of DEVELOPMENT.

Acceptance angle

The 'angle of view' of an exposure meter. Too wide an acceptance angle can give a false reading, especially when taking a light reading in close-up. Meter designs use systems of simple lenses, baffles or condensors that limit the acceptance angle in order to increase effectiveness and standardize sensitivity.

Achromatic lens see ABERRATION

Actinic

Term used to describe the power of light to produce chemical or physical changes in materials exposed to it, for example photographic emulsions. The actinic quality of lightwaves is stronger at the blue-violet end of the spectrum.

Actinometer

See HURTER & DRIFFIELD
Early type of exposure meter that calculated with a fair degree of accuracy the ACTINIC effect of incident light. Some were designed in the form of a fob watch, others – such as Watkin's Actinometer – as a brass cylinder with a series of adjustable scales. Each scale represented a different factor – sensitivity of the plate, type of subject, diaphragm aperture, value of the light. The latter

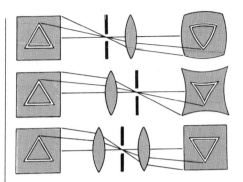

Barrel distortion (A) and pincushion distortion (B) can be minimized by a compound lens (C) with the aperture between the lens elements.

ABRASION MARKS

AGFA AG

AERIAL PERSPECTIVE

AGITATION SURGE MARKS

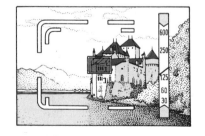

ALBADA FINDER

was calculated by exposing a strip of specially prepared silver bromide paper supplied with the instrument until it darkened to match the tint of a disc of 'average' tone, also supplied. The number of seconds taken to achieve this indicated the light value. Attached to the actinometer was a chain or cord with a weight at one end to form a seconds pendulum, which made timing easier. When the various scales were adjusted in succession to the value of each factor, a pointer indicated the exposure. Photographers working in a studio, and in lower levels of light, would use the more sensitive Watkin's 'indoor meter.' Bear in mind that these instruments were invented at a period when photographic plates often required exposures of up to 2 minutes.

Acutance
Scientific measurement of image sharpness. It is determined by testing how rapidly tones change from light to dark on a contact-printed image of a knife edge; the more rapid the transition, the sharper the image. Acutance, together with RESOLVING POWER, plays an important part in subjective assessments of a photograph's clarity of definition.

Additive synthesis
Means of producing a colour image by mixing blue, green and red coloured lights in proportion to those reflected by the original subject. This synthesis was first demonstrated in 1861 by the Scottish scientist JAMES CLERK MAXWELL. He made three positive black and white transparencies of a tartan ribbon taken through separate primary filters, then projected them through primary filters on to a white screen, so producing the world's first colour photograph. When the additive primaries are combined in pairs, they give the primaries used in the SUBTRACTIVE SYNTHESIS: blue/green make cyan; blue/red make magenta; red/green make yellow. A form of additive synthesis was used in early colour photography procedures such as the AUTOCHROME and is used today in colour television, but since the 1920s colour photography has been based essentially on the subtractive synthesis.

Agfa AG
Leading German manufacturer of films and pioneer makers of colour film on a large scale. Agfa introduced the Agfa Colour screen plate in 1916, an additive material that gave a transparency. They followed this in 1932 with Agfa Colour Lenticulated Film, and were close rivals with Kodak for the first SUBTRACTIVE INTEGRAL TRIPACK FILM.

Aerial perspective
Phenomenon created by haze or mist in the atmosphere, causing distant parts of a landscape to appear blue and softened. It is produced by the scattering of short (blue) lightwaves that refract and reflect droplets of moisture (mist) or dust (haze) particles in the air. The effects of aerial perspective can be very attractive visually and help to convey a sense of depth, but where clarity is essential, UV and skylight filters can penetrate haze but not mist.

Agitation
Technique in processing where the solution is kept in motion in order to ensure uniform development and fixing of the material.

Air bells
Bubbles of air which form on the surface of films or papers during DEVELOPMENT. They appear if the processing chemicals are not agitated sufficiently, and leave spots on the emulsion. A WETTING AGENT in the developer helps to prevent air bells from forming by reducing surface tension.

Airbrush

Instrument that uses compressed air to spray paint in a very fine mist. In appearance it is rather like a large fountain pen and is held in a similar manner, with the forefinger controlling the supply of air. The airbrush can be used for colouring photographs, retouching positives and negatives, hiding the joins in montaged photographs, adding pictorial effects such as clouds in a landscape, and removing defects or unwanted backgrounds. The techniques of successful airbrushing are not easy to master, but they make possible effects that are difficult and often impossible to obtain with even the finest brush.

Airbrushing

Airbrushing consists of three steps. First, dry-mount the print and cover the picture area with clear, self-adhesive masking film, taking care not to trap air bubbles. Then, using a sharp scalpel, cut around the outline of the main subject and peel off the masking film. Starting with a broad spray, build up the colour. To create a soft edge, constantly move a card mask cut to the appropriate shape over the print surface while airbrushing around it. Airbrushing was used to create the rainbow in the print far right. A thin sliver of mask was cut away and, with the airbrush about 4cm above the print, red pigment was sprayed on in a band. The next sliver of mask was removed and orange sprayed on while a card mask was used to shield the red band. This sequence was repeated for the additional colours.

Albada finder

Type of direct-vision VIEWFINDER in which the area of the subject that will be recorded on the film is indicated by white framing lines. The viewfinder's ANGLE OF VIEW is greater than that of the lens, so part of the subject is seen outside the frame. The framing lines on the inner surface of the rear window of the finder are reflected in the curved half-silvered mirror which forms the front window.

Alkali

Chemical with the property of neutralizing acids, and having a pH value above 7. Alkalis, such as sodium hydroxide, are used in developers to adjust the pH to a suitable level.

Alum

Double sulphate of aluminium and potassium and used as a hardener in photographic processing, mainly in fixing baths. There are several varieties: Chrome Alum (potassium chromium sulphate); aluminium potassium sulphate, and potash alum (potassium aluminium sulphate) – common alum.

Ambrotype

A variation of the COLLODION process which yielded a positive picture directly, without an intermediate printing stage. Ambrotypes were deliberately underexposed COLLODION negatives on a glass support, with a black backing that served to create a positive effect by reversing the tones.

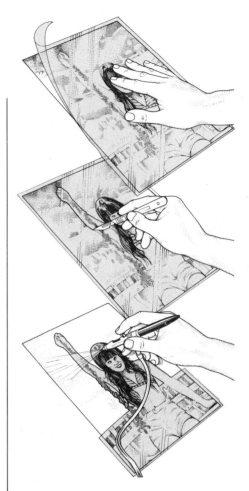

AIRBRUSHING: Photographs and other forms of artwork can be skilfully retouched by airbrushing.

AMBROTYPE

ANDRESEN, MOMME

ANGLE OF VIEW *The focal length of a lens determines its angle of view. A wide angle lens, typically 24mm to 35mm, gives a panoramic view; a telephoto lens (135mm plus) brings distant objects close up.*

Ammonia

A compound of nitrogen and hydrogen. Several by-products and compounds of ammonia, especially the salts, are used in photographic processes: ammonium carbonate is used as an alkali in developers, ammonium chloride (sal ammoniac) is used in toners and some bleachers; ammonium hydroxide in some developers and intensifiers, ammonium persulphate is a proportional reducer; ammonium sulphide used as a toner and intensifier, ammonium thiosulphate, a powerful fixing agent used in rapid fixing solutions.

Anamorphic lens

Lens that uses prisms or cylindrical elements to produce an image with a wider angle of view in the horizontal direction than the vertical, or vice versa. The image thus looks stretched or squashed, and can be restored to its normal aspect by printing or projection through a similar lens. Anamorphic lenses are particularly associated with motion pictures, as they can compress a wide-angle view on to a standard frame of film, which gives a wide-screen effect (such as Cinemascope) when projected. In still photography they are used mainly for trick effects.

Anastigmat

Lens corrected for astigmatism – the inability of a lens to focus vertical and horizontal lines in the same focal plane. See PROTAR LENS.

Anastigmatic lens

Lens corrected for the ABERRATION of astigmatism.

Andresen, Momme

German research chemist, director of Agfa and discoverer of the important amino compound developers.

Angle of view

The angle over which a lens accepts

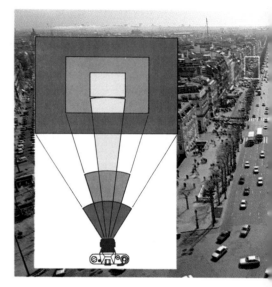

light or 'sees'. On a 35mm camera a standard 50mm lens has an angle of view of about 45°, roughly equivalent to normal human vision. (By 'normal human vision' is meant the angle over which our eyes see a clearly focused image; overall angle of human vision is about 150°–170°, but what we see at the periphery of our vision is indistinct. Our angle of vision seems to be more than that of a standard lens because in practice our eyes are continually moving, and our brains processing the information into an overall picture; to stare fixedly ahead like the 'eye' of a camera is completely unnatural.) A 28mm lens has an angle of view of about 73° and a 135mm lens one of about 20°. Angle of view can be expressed more scientifically as the angle subtended by the diagonal of the film or focal plane at the rear NODAL POINT of the lens. Thus the larger the negative format, the greater the angle of view for any particular focal length. On a large-format camera, for example, a 50mm lens will give a wide-angle view, not a standard one, and on a camera using 120 roll-film, a standard lens has a focal length of about 80mm. Similarly, a standard lens for a camera taking 110 film has a focal length of about 24mm.

Ansco

An American company associated with Agfa prior to World War II. They manufactured a reversal tripack called Ansco Color, practically identical to Agfacolor, and launched it in America in 1942, mainly for the military. After the war it was renamed Anscochrome.

Ångstrom unit

Unit by which wavelengths of light are measured. One unit, abbreviated Å, measures one ten-millionth of a millimetre (10^{-6} mm).

Anhydrous

Term which indicates that a substance is free from water, used in photography particularly to distinguish a chemical in powder form from the same substance when hydrated.

Animation

A series of progressive pictures – drawings or photographs – designed to convey movement and action. The pictures may be produced on film and projected, as in movie cartoons, or bound together in sequence as a 'flick book'.

Anti-halation backing

Coating of dye or pigment on the back of negative materials that absorbs the light that passes through the emulsion. Without this backing, light could reflect back through the emulsion, causing 'halos' around the highlights.

Anti-Newton see NEWTON'S RINGS

Antioxidant

A chemical, used principally in developing, to slow down the rate of oxidization. A typical example is sodium sulphite.

Anti-reflection coating see COATED LENS

*The picture **above**, taken from the top of the Arc de Triomphe, Paris, is a detail from the wide-angle shot, **above left**. Enlarging a detail gives the same effect as increased focal length where depth appears compressed.*

Aperture

Opening at the front of a camera which admits light. It is usually circular, and except in very simple cameras is variable in size, so regulating the amount of light that passes through the lens to the film. The term EFFECTIVE APERTURE is used to indicate the diameter of the beam of light that passes through the outer lens component along its axis to the aperture. Except in the unusual circumstances of the aperture being in front of the lens, the effective aperture is slightly larger than the real aperture, as the light is refracted as it enters the lens and thus the beam is narrowed. The effective aperture, however, increases or decreases proportionally as the real aperture is varied, usually by means of an iris diaphragm. RELATIVE APERTURE is the ratio of the focal length of the lens to the effective aperture. Thus, if the lens has a focal length of 50mm and the effective aperture is 25mm, the relative aperture is $50/25 = 2$. This is commonly expressed as an f number, in this case f2; the larger the f number the smaller the aperture. The usual sequence marked on the lens barrel is 2, 2.8, 4, 5.6, 8, 11, 16, 22, each 'stop' marking (approximately) a halving of the amount of light which the aperture admits. Some lenses go outside this range, and a lens with a large maximum relative aperture is referred to as 'fast' because the amount of light is can transmit to the film makes shorter exposure possible – a very useful feature in dim lighting conditions and/or when high shutter speeds are required, as, for example, in indoor sports photography. The current state of lens design and manufacture determines the standards by which a lens is considered fast for its focal length. Today a standard 50mm lens with a wider maximum aperture than f2 or a 28mm or 135mm lens with a wider maximum aperture than f2.8 could be described as such. The greater the 'speed' of a lens, the more difficult (and thus more expensive) it is to manufacture.

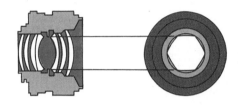

*APERTURE: How aperture effects depth of field. At the widest setting (**above and right**) the depth of field, or zone of sharp focus, is shallow.*

Stopped down halfway, the sharpness increases.

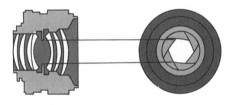

Stopped right down to the smallest aperture (f/16 or f/22) the depth of field extends from just in front of the camera to infinity. (see also DEPTH OF FIELD).

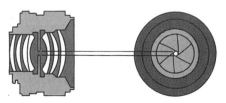

Exposure related to aperture.
At f/2

An open aperture emphasises
the subject by rendering the
background out of focus.

f/3.5

f/5.6

As you stop down, foreground
begins to blend with the
middle distance.

f/8

f/11

With a closed aperture, the
entire picture area is in focus.
This technique of stripping
down to achieve selective
focus, depends on the nature
of the subject and area of
interest.

f/16 same shutter speed
throughout.

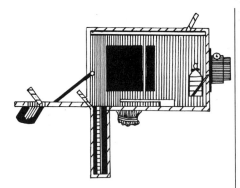

ARCHER'S CAMERA

AUTOFOCUS COMPACT CAMERAS

Aperture preference/priority see AUTOMATIC EXPOSURE

Apochromatic lens see ABERRATION

Arc lamp
Lamp using as its source of illumination incandescent particles produced when an electric current passes across a gap (arc) in a circuit.

Archer, Frederick Scott
English inventor of the COLLODION PROCESS and of the AMBROTYPE. Archer's invention, like the negative/positive process of FOX TALBOT, was of a fundamental nature. It reduced exposure times in portraiture from minutes to seconds and encouraged the use of glass plates rather than a paper support, as had been previously used in Talbot's CALOTYPE. Archer was born in Bishops Stortford, Herts, in 1813 – ten years before NIEPCE'S first photograph. He became a numismatist, then a sculptor, working in London. Using photographs to provide reference work for his portrait busts, Archer learned the calotype process, and gradually drifted from the pursuit of sculpture to that of photographic research. He collaborated with a colleague, Peter Fry, to invent the AMBROTYPE. Archer died in poverty in 1857.

Artificial light
Term used to describe any light used in photography other than that from natural sources (usually the sun). Generally it refers to light specially set up by the photographer such as flash or floodlights. There is a difference in the sensitivity of emulsions to daylight and artificial light, and films may be rated for either type.

ASA
Abbreviation for American Standards Association, used to designate one of the most commonly used rating systems for FILM SPEED.

Aspheric lens
Lens where the surface curvature does not form part of a sphere, designed to eliminate spherical ABERRATION. One aspheric lens may replace two or more spherical elements, and thus simplify lens design.

Astigmatism see ABERRATION

Atmospheric perspective see AERIAL PERSPECTIVE

Auto-change timer
An electronic automated device used in slide projectors to feed a slide in at preselected intervals.

Autochrome
An ADDITIVE screen plate patented by the Lumière brothers, August and Louis, and launched in 1907. Autochromes were the first mass-produced colour plates, each plate a mosaic of microscopic grains of potato starch dyed orange-red, green, and blue-violet, which acted as colour filters. The plates were varnished and coated with a panchromatic emulsion. Although slow, and lacking in CONTRAST, they could produce photographs of a fine and delicate quality.

Auto-loading
System in automated cameras that feeds the leader of the film on to the take-up spool, and powered by the camera's batteries.

Automatic diaphragm see EXPOSURE METER

Automatic exposure
System that automatically sets correct exposure by linking a camera's exposure meter with the shutter or aperture or both. There are three main types: aperture priority or preferred, when the photographer sets the aperture and the camera selects the appropriate speed; shutter priority or

preferred, when the photographer chooses the speed and the camera sets the correct aperture; and programmed, when the camera sets both aperture and shutter speed. Multi-mode cameras can be set to aperture or shutter priority, and, in some models, programmed. Aperture priority is advantageous when it is important to control depth of field; shutter priority comes into its own particularly in action photography; and programmed exposure can be useful when the photographer has to react quickly to get a 'grab shot'.

Automatic focusing/Autofocus see also FOCUSING

Method of automatically focusing the camera or enlarger without intervention from the photographer, as distinct from focus indication, where the photographer turns the focusing ring until a display indicates that the point of sharpest focus has been reached. There are two basic types of autofocus system: active and passive. In active systems the camera emits a signal – usually either ultrasound, or infrared radiation – and measures some function of the returning signal in order to judge subject distance. In passive systems, components in the camera actually judge image sharpness, not subject distance. Ultrasonic autofocus is presently used only on instant cameras: a transducer emits a high-pitched chord of sound frequencies, and the time taken for the echo to return indicates to the camera the subject distance (rather like a sonar depth finder on a ship), so that a motor can adjust the lens for optimum sharpness. Most compact 35mm viewfinder cameras use infrared autofocus. Here a mirror linked to the lens directs a beam of infrared across the scene in a scanning action as the lens moves outwards from close-focus settings towards an infinity setting. A forward-looking infrared detector detects a maximum of reflected IR

when the beam crosses a centrally placed subject, and at this point the movement of the lens is arrested, and the shutter released. Passive autofocus systems are mostly used in SLRs and rely on light-sensitive detectors in the focal plane.

When the image is unsharp, signals from each detector will be broadly similar, but as the lens is moved towards the position of sharpest focus, the contrast of the image at the focal plane increases, and the signals from the detectors diverge – some strengthen, some get weaker. The camera judges the image to be in focus when the differences between the signals reach a maximum. No autofocus system is foolproof: ultrasound systems cannot focus through glass, infrared systems are misled by highly IR-absorbent subjects, and passive systems do not work well at low ambient light levels. Autofocus enlargers work on a quite different principle. The lens-to-negative distance necessary for sharp focus is linked by a simple formula to the focal length of the enlarger lens and to the degree of enlargement. So a mechanical linkage operated by a precisely-machined cam can change the distance from lens to negative as the enlarger head is moved up and down.

Autowinder see MOTOR-DRIVE

Axis

Theoretical line passing through the centre of a lens along which light waves travel in a straight line. The optical axis of a lens is where surface curvature (and therefore refraction) is at a minimum.

AUTOMATIC EXPOSURE

AVAILABLE LIGHT

B

B setting

Setting on the shutter speed dial of
cameras at which the shutter remains
open as long as the shutter button is
held down, allowing for longer
exposures than the preset speeds on
the camera. The 'B' stands for 'bulb'.

BACK PROJECTION

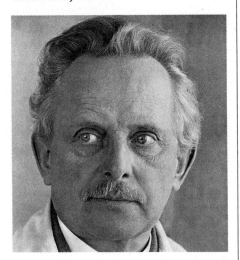

BARNACK, OSCAR

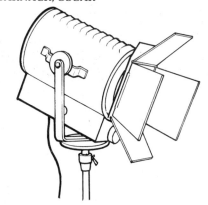

BARN DOOR

Back focus

The distance between the back surface of a lens and the FOCAL PLANE when the lens is focused on infinity. In a simple one-element lens, this will be virtually equivalent to the FOCAL LENGTH, and as a general rule back focus will vary proportionately with focal length. Many compound lenses, however, are designed so that the back focus is greater or lesser than the norm; a wide-angle lens for an SLR, for example, has a back focus much greater than the focal length to allow the mirror to operate freely, and a telephoto lens has a much shorter back focus than its equivalent focal length to minimize its size.

Back lighting see page 22

Backlight control

Manual override facility on some cameras which compensates for underexposure of a back-lit (contre-jour) subject. A subject lit from behind, but photographed from the front poses problems of contrast, because a TTL METER is influenced by the strong light source and will underexpose the main subject. In effect, the meter says 'stop down' to allow for the brightness of the front illumination. But the narrow aperture fails to allow for the darker tones of the subject. A backlight control thus gives the necessary additional exposure.

Back projection

Projecting an image or picture on the back of a translucent screen to provide a suitable background for a subject placed in front of it. The technique is particularly useful in commercial photography, where a model or car, for example, can be shot against an exotic scene, thus saving the expense of going on location. Considerable skill is needed to match the foreground subject with the background so that there are no inconsistencies, particularly in lighting. Back projection is also used to show films and slides in situations where the projector cannot be situated in front of the screen.

Bag bellows

Short sleeve that can be used in place of concertina-type bellows on some large-format cameras. Concertina-type bellows are unable to compress totally, and bag bellows enable the lens to be brought closer to the focal plane to focus the image from short focal length (wide-angle) lenses.

Barbero, Danielo

Probable inventor of the diaphragm at some time in the mid-16th century. The diaphragm constricted the light rays entering the CAMERA OBSCURA and so sharpened the image and improved the definition by concentrating the passage of light waves near the lens AXIS.

Bare bulb

Lighting technique used indoors where the aim is to produce very natural-looking results using FLASH. The flash unit is used without a reflector, so that the subject is lit both by direct light from the flash unit and by light reflected from the walls and ceiling of the room.

Barnack, Oscar

German camera technician who invented the LEICA. In the early 1900s Barnack pursued the idea of a lightweight and portable camera using reduced format film – *'klein negativ, grosse bild'*, 'small negative, big picture'. Barnack used 35mm motion picture film and standardized it for the still camera at 24mm × 36mm. He adapted from a movie camera project he was currently engaged in, and produced – in a specially-designed lightweight camera body – the first LEICA. Thus Barnack is considered by many to be the father of modern 35mm photography.

Barn doors
Hinged flaps mounted on the front of spotlights to control the direction of light and width of the beam.

Barrel distortion see ABERRATION

Baryta coating
Smooth, chemically inert base of barium sulphate in gelatin, used as the foundation layer for the emulsion on most types of fibre-based printing paper.

Base
The main support for the photographic emulsion, usually glass, cellulose triacetate, polyester or paper.

Bas-relief
Darkroom technique where a negative image and its positive counterpart, both on sheet film, are sandwiched slightly off-register in an enlarger or contact frame, producing in the developed print an image appearing as though side-lit and in low-relief.

BAS RELIEF Above and below

Back lighting

Lighting, natural or artificial, from behind the subject of a photograph. Because contrast tends to be high, judgement of exposure can be difficult in back-lit scenes. An average exposure meter reading over the whole scene will often produce over- or underexposure, so it is advisable to take also a separate reading for the part of the subject for which normal exposure is required. As well as causing problems, back lighting can also be used creatively, to give, for example, pure silhouetted shapes or a halo effect around a sitter's head in portraiture.

BACKLIGHTING: *Also known as CONTRE JOUR, backlit shots need carefully measured exposures. Foreground subjects can be frontally lit by fill in flash, or by reflectors, to compensate for the contrast.*

BATCH NUMBERS

BEAM SPLITTER

BECQUEREL, EDMOND

Batch numbers

Set of numbers printed on the packs of photographic papers and film to indicate a specific batch of emulsion coating. The numbers are important because of the slight variations in contrast and speed that may occur from batch to batch. With colour printing paper, filtration recommendations are also included, and these should be observed when progressing to a fresh batch.

Bayard, Hippolyte

Pioneer in the 1830s of direct positive pictures on silver chloride paper. His experiments were comparable to those of FOX TALBOT, whose paper negatives gradually obtained greater acceptance.

Bayonet see LENS MOUNT

Beaded screen

Type of front projection screen. The surface of the screen is covered with minute glass beads giving a brighter picture than a plain white screen, each bead acting as a tiny lens thus concentrating the light rays.

Beam splitter

Prism or prism and mirror system designed to split a beam of light into two or more separate beams. It is used in projectors to produce a stereoscopic image where the beam is split by a 90° prism, each separate image being then conveyed through additional prisms, so placed that they superimpose the images in register on the screen. An image-separating attachment can be used on the lens of a camera to produce side-by-side images on the film for stereo projection. Beam splitters are also used in cine and TV cameras, and in holography.

Becquerel, Edmond

One of the first experimenters (1848) of the coloured image using hydrous chloride stabilized by electrolysis. Becquerel immersed his plates in hydrochloric acid and silver chloride and deposited a thin film of silver by means of an electric current passing through the solution. The technique proved a satisfactory means of recording the spectral colours. The plates were not colour photographs, but they were a step in the right direction.

Bellows see EXTENSIONS

Between-the-lens see SHUTTER

Bennett, Charles

English amateur photographer whose improved GELATIN dry plate eventually rendered obsolete the wet COLLODION technique. At an exhibition in 1878 Bennett showed photographs of figures captured in movement. This was previously difficult owing to the 3-second-long exposure typical of wet plates, although some degree of success had been achieved by ENGLAND with his invention of the FOCAL PLANE SHUTTER in 1861, Bennett 'ripened' his gelatin plates by heating the emulsion, mixed with an excess of potassium bromide, at a temperature of 90°F from two to seven days, according to the desired degree of sensitivity. In spite of the extra sensitivity – or perhaps because of it – the plates were not a commercial success; photographers, accustomed to the slow wet plates, tended to overexpose their photographs.

Bichromated gelatin

Basic ingredient of the CARBON PROCESS which uses gelatin treated with potassium bichromate, a pigment and oxidizing agent. The search for permanent and practical photographic emulsion was a preoccuaption among amateur photographers of the mid-19th century, to which scientists also contributed useful discoveries. It was Mungo Ponton who observed in 1839 that potassium bichromate is light-sensitive, and later FOX TALBOT found that gelatin and other organic substances, treated with potassium bichromate, hardened when exposed to light in proportion to the exposure, and also became insoluble in water. The unexposed areas, remaining soluble, could then be washed away. A French chemist, Alphonse Poitevin, introduced carbon as a pigment to bichromated gelatin, spread it on to paper and exposed it in contact with a negative. The exposed areas of the treated gelatin hardened, the unexposed areas remained soluble and could be washed away with water. Poitevin patented his process in 1855, and an improved process in 1860. The most successful carbon process was introduced by the inventor Sir Joseph Wilson Swan in 1866, and made on a commercial scale. Swan's Newcastle-on-Tyne factory produced carbon gelatin tissues which had first to be sensitized with potassium bichromate and exposed under a negative. The next step required the tissue to be soaked in warm water to release the paper backing; the water also washed away the soluble areas, leaving the gelatin image to be dried, reversed, and placed on a support. The final image was in fact a relief – tones were represented by the thickness and density of the pigmented tissue.

Black body
Theoretically perfect source of radiant energy, used as a standard in measuring COLOUR TEMPERATURES or the spectral composition of light. Units of light, relating to the radiant energy of a light source, were originally measured by the luminous intensity of a candle (candle power or CANDELA) made according to standard specification. This method was superseded by the use of a black, hollow metal sphere that in theory reflected no light and that, when heated through red to orange, and finally to white (the melting point of platinum) emitted light purely as

radiant energy and thus gave a perfect, source of measurable luminance.

Bleaching
Chemical process that converts the black metallic silver of a photographic image into an almost colourless compound such as a SILVER HALIDE, which can then be dissolved, reduced or dyed. Bleaching is a preliminary stage in toning or intensification processes and is also used in most colour chemical developments.

Bleach-out process
Technique of producing a line drawing based on a photographic image. The outlines of a photograph are drawn over with pencil or waterproof ink, then the silver image is bleached away, leaving the outline behind. For best results, the subject represented should have clear outlines and the print should be fairly pale.

Blind
Also called a hide, a disguised or camouflaged cover or portable structure used to conceal a photographer while shooting wildlife.

Blix
Two-in-one processing bath, a bleach and fix combination used in rapid colour processing.

Blocking out
Painting out unwanted areas of a negative or print.

Bloomed lens
Alternative term for COATED LENS

Blur see page 26

Boom light
Studio light attached to a long horizontal pole, counterbalanced at the other end. It is used when a light on a conventional stand would intrude into the picture area, as, for example, when top lighting a portrait.

BLIND

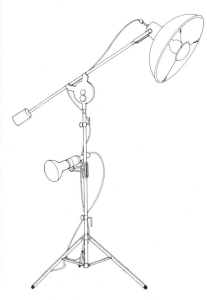

BOOM LIGHT

Blur

Unsharp or ill-defined image caused by a moving subject, camera shake, unclear focusing or lens aberration. Blur is often unintentional and undesirable, but can be used to creative effect. In particular, it is one of the photographer's principal means of creating a sense of movement. There are two main ways in which blur is used in this way: by choosing a shutter speed too slow to 'freeze' a moving subject, in which case it will appear blurred; or by 'panning' with a moving subject so that it is sharp while the background is blurred. Depending on the shutter speed chosen and hence the degree of blur, effects can be gained ranging from vivid action reportage, through various degrees of self-expression, to pure abstraction. Suitably long exposures of water in movement can produce particularly striking blurred effects. Blurring also occurs in those areas of a photograph outside the DEPTH OF FIELD zone, and this can be put to use in DIFFERENTIAL FOCUSING.

BRACKETING

Bounced flash

Technique of softening the light from a flash source by directing it on to a ceiling, wall, board or similar reflective surface before it reaches the subject. The light is diffused at the reflecting surface, and there is a decrease in light power because of absorption there and because of the greater distance between light source and subject. Bounced flash is particularly used in portraiture, where direct flash is often harsh and unflattering and can cause RED-EYE. If the reflecting surface is coloured, this will affect the light, so white surfaces should always be used for bounced flash unless special colour effects are desired.

Bracketing

Technique of ensuring optimum exposure by taking several identical pictures of the same subject at slightly different exposure settings. Bracketing is used in tricky, non-average lighting situations (back-lit scenes, snowscapes, sunsets), particularly when the EXPOSURE LATITUDE of the film is small.

Brewster's angle

Maximum polarizing angle of a reflected incident ray of light from a non-metallic bright surface.

Brewster, Sir David

Scottish scientist and founder of photographic STEREOSCOPY. Although the science of stereo vision is due to the investigations of Sir CHARLES WHEATSTONE, who constructed mirror and prism viewers, it was Brewster who in 1851 made a practical stereoscope with lenses, and applied it to the relatively new science of photography. The potential of Brewster's device was recognized not by the British but by the French, and in particular the optical firm of Duboscq, who popularized Brewster's model, and produced sets of stereoscopic Daguerreotypes. The

success of the stereoscope was remarkable – it was the television of the Victorian age – and fame seems to have lent an extra dimension to Brewster's character, revealing a vindictive streak similar to that of his friend, FOX TALBOT. Brewster disputed Wheatstone's claim to the priority of stereoscopy and to the invention of the stereoscope, ignoring the fact that Wheatstone had actually published his findings in 1838. Perhaps the real acclaim should go to Jules Duboscq, who saw the great marketing possibilities of the instrument, and made for it for viewing the first transparencies.

Bright field

Method of illumination used in photomicrography that lights the specimen from below, causing it to be seen against a light background. It is particularly used with transparent or translucent specimens. See also DARK FIELD.

Brometching

High contrast positive print resembling etching or line drawing; also the name of the technique used to produce it. A normal bromide print is placed in an acid bath to burn out the highlights and remove any grey tones. The print is then fixed and washed.

Bromide paper

One of the most common types of photographic paper used for black and white prints, giving a completely neutral image colour. It derives its name from the silver bromide with which it is coated.

Bromoil process

Technique of applying oil-based colour pigments to a bleached, black and white bromide print made on a special bromoil paper. The gelatin emulsion can also be stripped off the backing paper and the image transferred by pressure to another base. Prints made by bromoil transfer have a distinctive delicate quality, but the bromoil process is very little used today as suitable materials are difficult to obtain.

Brownie camera

Simple box camera based on the highly successful KODAK No 1 roll-film camera of 1888. The Kodak's inventor, GEORGE EASTMAN, saw the need for a simple mass-produced camera that even a child could operate – this was to be the 'Brownie'. Sold for one dollar, the camera used film with a format of $1\frac{1}{2} \times 2$in (37×50mm), giving 12 exposures as opposed to the Kodak's 100 exposures. The advantage was that the negatives were rectangular whereas the Kodak pictures were circular. The Brownie had the additional novel feature of daylight-loading roll-film spool, a red celluloid window at the back of the camera to read off the number of each exposed picture, and an optional viewfinder. As the camera was designed for a youthful market, Kodak packaged the camera in a box decorated with pixies: the figures were based on the traditional Scottish Brownie of folklore. No doubt the name was also suggested by the camera's designer, Frank Brownell.

Bubble chamber photography

Photographic technique used in nuclear physics to record the performance and behaviour of ionizing particles (protons and electrons). The bubble chamber contains super-heated hydrogen through which the high-energy particles are fired at speeds approaching that of light. The particles boil as they pass through the heated hydrogen, releasing a trail of bubbles. These are photographed by synchronized electronic flash linked to two or three cameras in sequence.

Buffer

An ALKALINE salt such as sodium carbonate or borax added to developers in order to maintain alkalinity. Developers weaken as the bromide content increases due to the liberation of hydrobromic acid. A buffer is therefore added to maintain the pH value and the effective working life of the solution.

Bulk loader

Device for handling 35mm film that has been bought in bulk as a single length to be loaded into empty cassettes or special bulk film magazines that can replace the normal camera back. The loaders hold up to about 30m (100ft) of film, and any number of frames, to a maximum of about 36, can be loaded into the cassette. Bulk magazines hold up to 250 exposures and may have their own motor drive.

Burgess, John

London photographer who improved and made commercially available the first practical GELATIN dry plate, following the experiments of MADDOX. Burgess devised an emulsion of silver bromide and gelatin which he poured on to glass plates and allowed the plates to dry. These ready-made plates were first sold in 1873, but were not entirely satisfactory owing to the presence of silver crystalline salts, which impaired definition, and the dry plate awaited improvements from later experimenters.

Burning in or printing in

Technique used in printing photographs when a small area of the print requires more exposure than the rest. After normal exposure a card with a hole in it is held over the print, so that only the area below the hole (for example, a highlight which is too dense on the negative) receives further exposure. The hands may be used instead of a card, and, as with DODGING, card or hands are kept constantly moving to prevent harsh tonal transitions.

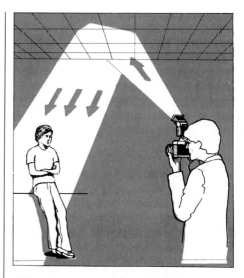

BOUNCED FLASH

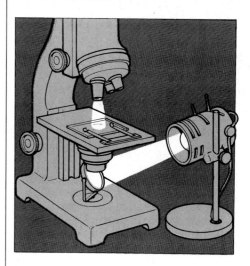

BRIGHT FIELD

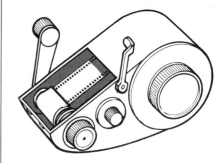

BULK LOADER

C

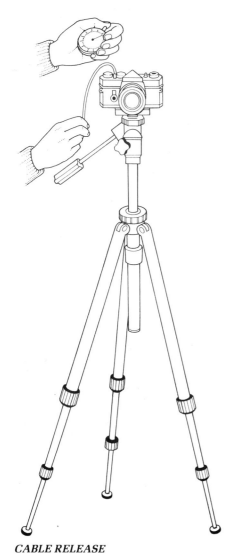

CABLE RELEASE

CALOTYPE

Cable release see REMOTE RELEASE
Thin cable encased in a flexible plastic or metal tube, used to fire the shutter without touching the camera. This helps to avoid CAMERA SHAKE when the camera is mounted on a tripod for a long exposure, or when it is fitted with a heavy long focal length lens. One end of the cable screws into a socket in the camera, often within the shutter release button; the other end has a plunger which when depressed fires the shutter. Some models have locking collars that hold the shutter open for long exposures, and some special equipment may have provision for several cable releases to operate at the same time, as for example when using bellows for close-up work. There is also a pneumatic type of release, operated by an air bulb, and fitted with a long cable, for remote control work, including self-portraiture. An air release is less liable to wear through friction, but will perish with age.

Callier effect
Scattering of light in a condenser-type enlarger, causing an increase in CONTRAST compared with the image formed from the same negative by a diffuser enlarger. When light rays from a condenser pass through a negative held in the carrier, they are selectively absorbed or scattered by the dense, high light areas, while passing unimpeded through the clear parts – the shadow areas. The effect is to give strong highlights and dense shadows. With a diffuser enlarger, the light reaching the negative has already been scattered by the diffuser itself, so no more scattering takes place. The Callier effect is named after the Belgian physicist André Callier, who first investigated it in 1909.

Calotype
Name given by FOX TALBOT (calotype from *kallos*, Greek word meaning beautiful) to the negative/positive photographs which he invented and patented. Calotypes, later more widely known as 'Talbotypes', were made by treating sheets of paper with a solution of silver iodide, followed by a solution of silver nitrate and gallic acid. The paper was exposed in the camera for a few minutes to obtain a latent image, which was again washed with gallo-nitrate of silver, and fixed with sodium thiosulphate (hypo). The dried negative was then contact printed in a frame on to silver chloride paper and exposed to strong sunlight. In 1844 Talbot published a six-part series 'The Pencil of Nature' illustrated with Calotype prints. There were other claimants to the neg/pos process, if not to the actual invention, at least to synchronaeity, by Hippolyte Bayard and the Bavarian photographers Kobell and Steinheil.

Camera

Light-proof precision apparatus incorporating a lens or a SHUTTER, and film transport mechanism or detachable MAGAZINE to hold film. Light, admitted through the lens, conveys an image on to the film for the process of PHOTOGRAPHY.

Camera movements see page 32

Camera obscura

Literally 'dark room' or 'dark chamber'. An ancient system of observing images transmitted by light through a small hole in a darkened room. By applying the principle to a portable tent or box and fitting the box with a lens to brighten the image, the device could be employed as an aid to drawing, especially in solving the problems of perspective. By and by, the camera obscura acquired such refinements as adjustable focus lenses, an opal glass screen to receive the projected image, and a mirror set at an angle of 45° to the lens, thus introducing the first REFLEX system. The camera obscura embodied all the fundamental characteristics of the modern camera with the exception of aperture and shutter.

Camera shake

Accidental movement of the camera during exposure, resulting in overall blurring of the photographic image. The main causes are pressing the shutter release too vigorously and hand-holding the camera while shooting at slow shutter speeds, especially with long focus lenses. Using a tripod and cable release will generally overcome the problem, but not, for example, when photographing near a source of vibration, such as heavy machinery on a factory floor. The slowest speed at which it is safe to

CAMERA OBSCURA

CAMERA SHAKE

Camera movements

Mechanical systems on large-format cameras that allow the relative positions of the lens and film to be adjusted. The movements can create greater DEPTH OF FIELD in specific planes, and can correct or distort image shapes as required, for example correcting converging verticals in architectural subjects. On SLR cameras similar but more restricted movements, generally limited to rising, falling and lateral movement, can be obtained by using a SHIFT LENS.

CAMERA MOVEMENTS: A wide-angle or standard lens will cause distortion of vertical lines, particularly noticeable in architectural shots, making buildings appear as if they were falling over backwards. Verticals can be corrected, as on the right, by altering the front and back panels of a view camera, or the SHIFT LENS of an SLR.
Depth of field can be increased, (above, right) by tilting the front lens panel (see SCHEIMPFLUG PRINCIPLE)

CARTES DE VISITE

hand-hold a camera varies with numerous factors, such as the weight of the camera, the smoothness of the shutter release mechanism and the skill and confidence of the photographer. Non-reflex cameras are slightly less susceptible to shake than SLRs because they do not have a mirror mechanism – a source of vibration. The use of long and heavy lenses will increase the effects of camera shake at slow shutter speeds, as will photographing in a moving vehicle by land, sea or air. Camera shake probably ruins more photographs than any other basic error, but it can also be used creatively, particularly in colour photography, where it can 'spread' the image.

Canada balsam

Fluid resin from a species of North American fir tree, used in lens manufacture to cement elements of optical glass together. It possesses a refractive index almost identical to that of glass and thus forms an invisible adhesive. Some manufacturers object to Canada balsam on the grounds that it yellows with age, but it takes at least 30 years before starting to discolour, and even then its effect will generally be negligible in black and white photography.

Candela

Unit of measurement used to indicate the strength of a light source. One candela (formerly known as one candle power) is defined as 1/60 of the luminous intensity of one square centimetre of a BLACK BODY at the solidification temperature of platinum (1,769°C).

Candle metre

Unit of measurement of illumination. It is defined as the illumination per square metre of a surface one metre from a point light source of one candela.

Capacitor flashgun

Flashgun incorporating a condenser (capacitor) that builds up a charge of electricity to fire an expendable flash bulb.

Carbon process see also DYE TRANSFER

Carbon printing was one of the most important and fundamental processes arising from the subtractive synthesis of colour photography. The process was made commercially viable by Sir Joseph Wilson Swan in 1864 using BICHROMATED GELATINE containing powdered carbon. The carbon tissues, a gelatine coating on paper, were sensitized by treating them with potassium bichromate. Swan improved the existing bichromated gelatine technique by making the tissue separable from its paper base by soaking in water. The tissues, exposed under a negative, could be tinted with aniline dyes in the colours cyan, magenta and yellow – the subtractive primaries – and put in register on a suitable base. The carbon process led to other developments such as Thomas Manly's Ozobrome process of 1905, also known as the Carbro Process. Here, the gelatin tissue hardened when in contact with silver bromide in proportion to the density of the silver and without exposure to light. Images could be transferred from a dyed gelatine tissue on to a bromide paper by pressing them in contact. The harder the gelatin the less dye was transferred, thus were tonal variations achieved. The silver then bleached away, leaving a positive relief image. These coloured tissues also led to a variety of processes such as the Lumière brothers patent of 1895; the Sanger Shepherd process of 1899; Leon Didier's Pinatype process of 1903, and Donisthorpe's process of 1907. These techniques of dye transfer are also known as imbibition printing.

Carbon tetrachloride
Solvent that may be used for cleaning the surface of negatives. It must be used in a well-ventilated atmosphere as its fumes are toxic.

Cartes de visite
Photographic visiting cards popularized by Andre Disderi in 1859 but probably invented by two French amateur photographers, Benjamin Delessert and Count Aguado. The Carte de visite was a photograph mounted on card, usually a full-length portrait but sometimes a multiple portrait, sometimes head and shoulders, or even views and landscapes. According to the story, Disderi, a fashionable Parisian photographer, was commissioned by Napoleon III, who asked Disderi to make one of his popular multiple portraits – ten shots on one plate. From the sitting, the Emperor had the portrait made into a visiting card – although it is hard to imagine that the head of an Empire would ever need a

visiting card. Disderi became famous overnight, progressed to become the richest photographer in France, if not in Europe, but died in poverty, in Nice. Among other prosperous cartes de visite photographers, were Mayall in England, Camille Silvy and Oliver Sarony.

Cartridge
Plastic film container, either 126 or 110 format. The film is wound from one spool to the take-up spool inside the sealed cartridge.

Cassette
Container for 35mm film. After exposure the film is wound from the camera's take-up spool, back into the cassette before the camera is opened.

Catadioptric lens see MIRROR LENS

Catalyst
Substance that influences the rate of a chemical reaction yet remains unchanged by the reaction. A catalyst is used, for example, in developers to increase the rate of OXIDATION.

Catch lights
The tiny highlights in the eyes of a subject in a portrait photograph, caused by the reflection of the light source.

Caustic potash
Alkaline chemical used in developers to accelerate development.

CC see also FILTERS
Abbreviation for Colour Correction filters.

CdS cell See also EXPOSURE METER
Photosensitive cell used in one type of light meter, incorporating a cadmium sulphide resistor, which regulates an electric current.

Centre-weighted meter
Type of TTL (through-the-lens) light

CASSETTE

CATCHLIGHTS

35

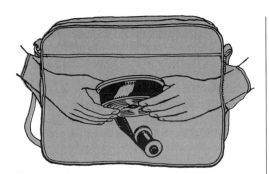

CHANGING BAG

CHANGING BAG

meter. The reading is most strongly influenced by the intensity of light at the centre of the image.

Changing bag
Bag made of opaque material and having elasticated sleeves that allows light-sensitive materials to be handled outside the darkroom. Bags for carrying cameras and equipment sometimes have a changing bag incorporated into them.

Characteristic curve see HURTER & DRIFFIELD
Graph of the image density produced by a photographic emulsion against the logarithm of the exposure. A black and white film has one curve, a colour film three – one for each layer of emulsion. The graphs give information about emulsion speeds, fog level, contrast and tone reproduction. A steep curve indicates a high-contrast material.

Chemical fog
Overall deposit of metallic silver on a negative, caused by overactive or incorrect developing solution or by certain reducing agents.

Chlorobromide papers
Printing papers coated with both silver bromide and silver chloride, used to produce warm tones in the image, when processed by normal development.

Chromatic aberration see
ABERRATION

Chrome alum (Chromium potassium sulphate)
Chemical that acts as a hardening ingredient in some fixing baths.

Chromogenic development
Term used to describe the simultaneous production of a colour image with a silver halide image, by means of a DYE COUPLER in the emulsion, or in the developing solution.

Chromographoscope
Device now of mainly historial interest and combining a camera and viewer employing ADDITIVE SYNTHESIS, where the image is obtained by mixing coloured lights, each light transmitting an identical image in one of the primary colours. The chromographoscope was patented in 1874, and was one of several similar systems designed by the pioneers of colour photography, such as Louis DUCOS DU HAURON's 'chromoscope' and FREDERICK IVES' 'Kromscop'. The device took three separation negatives on one plate, the image being transmitted via a series of mirrors through coloured filters to the viewing lens.

Chromogenic film
Recently introduced black and white material that has been hailed as one of the most important innovations in

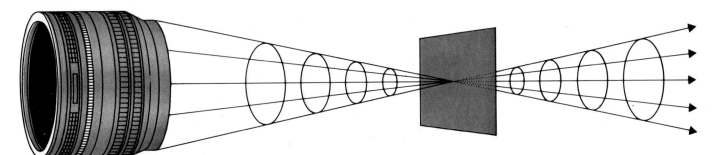

CIRCLES OF CONFUSION

monochrome emulsion technology of the 20th century. It forms a silver halide image in the usual way, but during processing the silver grains couple with image-forming dyes; the silver is then removed by bleaching, leaving a negative that is free of silver and consequently almost grainless. In practice, this means that a chromogenic film with a speed of ASA 400 can produce the sharpness of detail associated with conventional film rated at ASA 125. A drawback of chromogenic film is that its processing requires different chemistry and higher temperatures than conventional black and white film, but this is not likely to prove a handicap to those already working with colour materials, and many commercial processors handle chromogenic film. Ilford XP1 was the first chromogenic film to be launched, in 1980, followed by Agfapan Vario-XL.

Cibachrome

Colour print process introduced in Switzerland in 1963. It is based on the silver-dye-bleach principle originally proposed in 1905 by the Austrian KARL SCHNITZEL. A dye destruction TRIPACK of subtractive colours, Schnitzel's idea was revived and exploited by Bela Gaspar in 1930. Gaspar produced a subtractive tripack of positive dye images, the dyes being destroyed in proportion to the exposure during the development. In the Cibachrome process the exposed tripack is developed to produce three negative silver images. These are then bleached away leaving positive dye images in each layer.

Circle of confusion

Disc of light in the image produced by a lens when a point on the subject is not perfectly brought into focus. In fact, no lens can resolve a point as a point, but from normal viewing distance the human eye accepts a circle as a point if its diameter is less than

about 1/100in (0.25mm), and an image or parts of an image made up of circles of confusion smaller than this will appear sharp.

Cleaning or clearing bath

Any bath used in the processing of negatives or prints to remove stains or neutralize chemicals left by previous parts of the processing.

Coated lens

Lens in which the glass-to-air surfaces have been treated with an anti-reflection coating, such as magnesium fluoride, which reduces flare and increases light transmission. Most modern lenses are multi-coated.

Cold cathode enlarger

Type of non-condenser enlarger using as its light source a special fluorescent tube with a low working temperature. It provides even diffuse illumination and produces less contrasty prints than condenser enlargers (see CALLIER EFFECT). The uniformity of their illumination makes cold cathode enlargers very suitable for large-format work.

Collage see also PHOTOMONTAGE
Pictorial arrangement in which various items are juxtaposed to form a composition. These may include scraps of newsprint, photographs, pieces of fabric, wood, and so on, often incorporated with a painting on a panel or canvas.

Collodion process Historic photographic technique invented by FREDERICK SCOTT ARCHER employing a glass plate coated with collodion, a solution of cellulose nitrate (guncotton or pyroxylin) in a mixture of sulphuric ether and alcohol. Until Archer's invention, photographs were made on metal or paper, as in Fox Talbot's CALOTYPE process. For a successful calotype portrait the sitter had to remain perfectly still for up to *2*

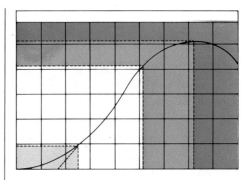

CHARACTERISTIC CURVE

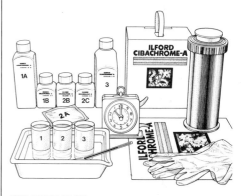

CIBACHROME

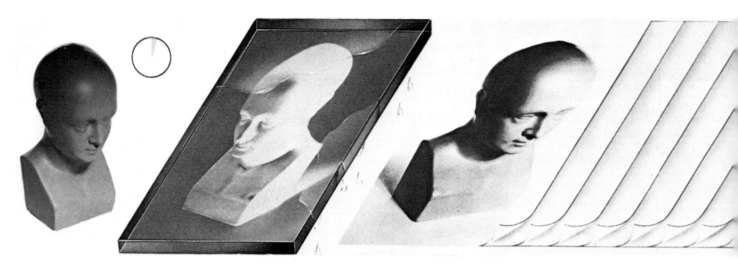

COLLODION PROCESS

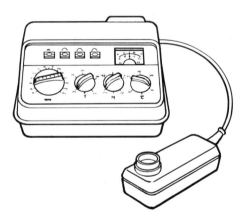

COLOUR ANALYSER

minutes while the exposure was made. Archer's process reduced exposure times to mere seconds. It had occurred to Archer that the newly-discovered substance collodion (by Ménard and Domonte in 1847, and called by them collodion from the Greek κολλα, meaning glue) might serve as a robust substitute for paper in the form of an emulsion spread on glass. The plate was first polished, then given a substratum of albumen to provide a key surface for the collodion. Before being poured on to the plate the collodion was mixed with potassium iodide and potassium bromide dissolved in alcohol. This produced a pourable substance that could be spread to make a thin, tough and transparent film. The plate was next sensitized by immersion in a bath of silver nitrate, distilled water and nitric acid, when it was immediately ready for exposure. The sensitizing stage converted the silver nitrate to silver bromide and iodide due to the action of potassium salts in the collodion. Archer's 'wet plate' process was revolutionary in spite of the limitations inherent in exposing wet slides in the camera. Keeping the emulsion wet was important because the silver iodide and bromide lost its sensitivity if allowed to dry, but in the wet state was highly sensitive. Furthermore, the dried silver salts formed visible crystals that impaired image definition, producing a pattern in the negative. The plates were developed in a solution of either pyrogallol or more frequently ferrous sulphate and acetic acid, and intensified with silver nitrate. Actually, the collodion development was really one of intensification since the process was physical rather than chemical (see DEVELOPER). The ferrous sulphate converted the silver salt to metallic silver, which formed a deposit on the exposed halides in the emulsion – a precipitate of iron and silver on the LATENT IMAGE. This image could be further intensified by adding silver nitrate to the developer. After development, the plate was fixed with hyposulphite of soda. It can be seen that the collodion process was messy and involved preparation and processing on the spot, but nonetheless the great advantage for portrait photographers – increased film speed – made it the only workable technique for 30 years until the invention of the gelatin dry plate.

Colour analyser
Darkroom device that measures the colour balance of a projected image and determines the correct exposure and filtration for making colour enlargements. Colour analysers are

fairly expensive pieces of equipment, but they save the time and paper that would be used in trial exposures.

Colorama
Large wide rolls of paper, coloured or black or white, used for seamless backgrounds in studio photography.

Colour correcting or light balancing filters
Comparatively weak colour filters used to correct for small differences between the colour temperature of the illumination used for a particular exposure and that for which the film was manufactured. The name is also sometimes rather loosely used to describe the cyan, magenta and yellow filters that are used in an enlarger to balance the colour of prints made from colour negatives.

Colour couplers see DYE COUPLERS

Colour developers
Highly active and concentrated CHROMOGENIC chemicals that develop both the silver image and the subtractive colour dyes in TRIPACK films. Where couplers are incorporated in the developers, the latent silver image is first developed; then the film is processed so that each colour layer is independently developed for the

production of dye images. The principal developing agents in negative and reversal films are salts of diethyl-paraphenylene diamine, potassium bromide and sodium carbonate.

Colour head
Enlarger head with 'dial-in' system of three filtration controls in cyan, yellow and magenta, which progressively mix the coloured lights in a mixing chamber to achieve the right degree of filtration in colour printing.

COLOUR HEAD

39

COMPACT CAMERA

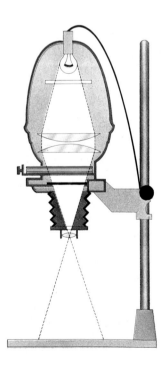

CONDENSER ENLARGER

Colour synthesis

The formation of colours by mixing lights, dyes or pigments of other colours. Colour photography depends on either ADDITIVE SYNTHESIS or SUBTRACTIVE SYNTHESIS.

Colour temperature

see also MIRED

Measurement of a light source's energy distribution over the SPECTRUM and hence its colour quality. Colour temperature is usually expressed in Kelvins (K), which are equivalent to degrees centigrade $+273°$, absolute zero being $-273°$ (0K). When a light source is said to have a particular colour temperature (say 5,000K), it means that a BLACK BODY would have to be heated to that temperature to emit radiation of the colour of the light source. A black body when heated to a certain temperature will begin to glow red, and as temperature increases it will become orange, and so on. Thus, light at the red end of the spectrum has a low colour temperature, and colour temperature becomes progressively

higher as light moves to the blue end of the spectrum. Colour temperature, then, has no necessary connection with actual temperature, and does not relate to the notion that red is a 'warm' colour and blue a 'cool' one. In colour photography, a colour reversal film must be matched or 'balanced' to the overall colour and luminance of the light to which it will be exposed. Most forms of artificial light have a colour temperature in the range of 2,000K to 6,000K; the colour temperature of blue sky with bright sunshine is about 6,000K, and of overcast sky about 10,000K.

Coma see ABERRATION

Combination printing

General term for techniques in which more than one negative is printed on to a single sheet of paper.

Compact camera

35mm camera with a direct-vision viewfinder and (usually) an autofocusing system. They are simple to operate pocket cameras of an extremely functional and compact design – hence the name. The more sophisticated models have auto wind and rewind, electronic self-timing, auto film speed setting, integral flash and metering.

Complementary colours

Any two colours that, when mixed, will produce an achromatic colour: white, grey or black. The complementary colour pairs used in most colour film and printing processes are red-cyan, green-magenta and blue-yellow.

Compur shutter

Between-the-lens, leaf type, or compound SHUTTER, first used with Zeiss lenses, and introduced by Frederick Deckel in 1912; the Compur was based on his original invention of 1904 – the compound shutter. This design employs spring-loaded metal leaves that form a central, variable opening (see SHUTTER) operated by clockwork regulators (escapements) to open and close the diaphragm. The shutter is dial-set, and reaches speeds of 1/250th to 1/300th second.

Computer flash see FLASH

Condenser
Lens, usually of simple construction, used in an enlarger or slide projector to concentrate light from the lamp source and focus it on the negative or slide.

Constant density ratio
Law stating that the relative SILVER HALIDE densities on an exposed negative are decided by the exposure, not by development, as development affects only contrast.

Contact print
A print made by direct contact with the NEGATIVE, exposed to light, and developed and fixed normally. A sheet of 'contacts' is usually a quick reference to a roll of developed negatives from which examples may be selected for subsequent enlargement.

Contrast
Areas of a subject or on a photograph of the subject that are markedly different in tone; the difference between HIGHLIGHT and SHADOW density. Contrast in a subject if affected by the intensity and direction of the light; the inherent brightness or darkness of the subject; the type of photographic material used in rendering the subject; the degree of development, and other factors. For example, fast panchromatic films that respond to highlight and shadow while compressing the more subtle medium tones in the picture, are said to be 'contrasty'.

CONTACT PRINT

CONTRAST

CONTRE JOUR *(see BACKLIGHTING)*

example – and created by the English designer Harold Taylor in 1893, when working with the York optical firm of Cooke. Many early lenses had limited correction for ABERRATIONS and worked well only at small apertures. The Ross Concentric of 1888 had a good degree of correction but worked at f16. Zeiss halved this with the PROTAR, a symmetrical anastigmat, at f8. In 1893 Taylor produced his novel arrangement, which had a maximum aperture of f4.5, later improved to f3.5. The Cooke Triplet consists of a double separated front element of positive and negative glasses, and a rear positive glass, with the diaphragm just behind the negative component. The negative (diverging) lens corrected astigmatism. To achieve this, the FOCAL LENGTH of the negative lens had to be equal to the focal length of the two positive lenses. The Cooke Triplet had a FIELD of 53° and was fast for its time, so the arrangement lent itself well to future development. It seems that the Cooke was not the first triplet design. Dallmeyer had produced one in 1860, free of distortion and with a reasonably flat field, but operating at f15.

Cosine law
Law relating to the variation in illumination between the centre and the edges of an image formed by a lens. At the edges of the image the lightwaves fall more obliquely on the negative and brightness is correspondingly decreased. The law states that the illumination varies as the fourth power of the cosine of the angle formed between the lens AXIS and an imaginary line drawn between the rear NODAL POINT and the image point in question.

Cove
Modular photographic background used in studios and for film sets. A cove is a curved, seamless backdrop hiding the points where walls meet the

Contre jour
Alternative term for BACKLIGHTING (French for 'against the light').

Cooke triplet lens
Fundamental lens type from which many modern lenses have been derived – the famous Zeiss Tessar lens, for

floor and ceiling. Coves are made of white polystyrene or glass fibre.

Covering power

The maximum area of the FOCAL PLANE over which a lens is capable of producing an image of acceptable illumination and definition. Illumination falls off progressively from the centre of the image in accordance with the COSINE LAW, and definition, because of ABERRATIONS, suddenly decreases at a certain point, earlier at wide apertures than small apertures. The covering power of a lens is normally only slightly greater than the negative size for which it is intended. In the case of a lens intended for use on a camera with CAMERA MOVEMENTS, however, covering power must be considerably greater in order to accommodate the differences in alignment between the lens and the film plane that the movements produce. Similarly, a SHIFT LENS must have greater covering power than an ordinary lens of the same focal length.

Cropping

Editing of a print or image, and the rejection of unwanted areas to concentrate more on the main subject of the picture.

Cros, Charles

With DUCOS DU HAURON, one of the inventors of the subtractive system. By a remarkable coincidence, Cros, French poet and amateur photographer, announced in 1869 his discovery at exactly the same time as du Hauron. Cros, du Hauron and IVES in America all had the same idea at more or less the same time, sponsored no doubt by previous experiments of other pioneers in photography. Like du Hauron, Cros was a theorist whose ideas had to await later technical progress. He designed a chromomètre colour analysis device, and also – independently – the imbibition technique of gelatine DYE TRANSFER.

CROPPING: A cropped picture concentrates the eye to the main area of

Cross front

Movable lens panel on some types of large-format cameras that allows the lens to move horizontally across the camera. This is one of the principal CAMERA MOVEMENTS.

Curvature of field see ABERRATION

Cut film

Another name for SHEET FILM.

Cyan

Blue-green colour, one of the three primaries used in SUBTRACTIVE SYNTHESIS.

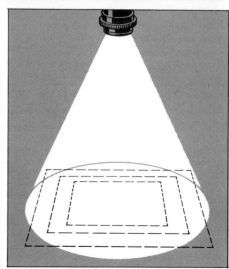

COVERING POWER

Daguerreotype

Early photograph made on a copper plate coated with silver and sensitized with silver iodide. The image was developed using mercury vapour, giving a direct positive. Louis Jacques Mande Daguerre's place in the history of photography is undisputed yet his invention was a by-product of mainstream photography, research and development. The Daguerreotype was a photographic, metallic visible image made positive by reflected, angled lightwaves: the picture was visible only when the shiny, unexposed areas of the plate reflected a black surface. Daguerre used polished silvered plates and sensitized them with iodine vapour, thus converting the surface of the plate to silver iodide. Exposure in the camera produced a latent image that could be 'developed' by exposing the plate to mercury vapour. This rendering visible of the latent image was a fundamental discovery in photography. In short, Daguerre discovered the all-important function of DEVELOPMENT. Minute particles of mercury conveyed in the vapour produced a mercury-silver amalgam which attached itself to those areas of the plate exposed to the light. The mercury particles were disposed over the image in proportion to the exposure. The unaffected areas of silver iodide were then removed in a bath of saline, then the plate was washed and dried, and sealed in a protective, airtight glass frame. Later experiments used a vapour of bromine and iodine to form silver bromide-silver iodide, making the plate more sensitive, and Daguerreotypes were additionally treated with gold chloride for improved image quality and permanence. Daguerre's invention was announced by the French scientist and politician François Arago in January 1839. The French government awarded Daguerre a pension of 6,000 francs and pressed him to publish details of the process.

DAGUERREOTYPE

Dark field
See also BRIGHT FIELD. Method of illumination used in photo-micrography which lights the specimen from above, causing it to be seen against a dark background.

Darkroom see page 46

Dark slide
Light-tight holder in which sheet film is loaded for exposure in the camera. Holders are often designed to take two sheets of film back to back; these are called double dark slides.

Data back
Device that can replace a normal back on an SLR to enable figures recording information to be optically imprinted on to the corner of the negative. A series of light-emitting diodes print the data on to the film at the moment of exposure. Data backs can be programmed to number each picture in sequence, to record the date or time, or even exposure details. Some units can imprint a one-line caption.

Daylight film
Colour reversal film balanced to give accurate colour rendering in average daylight, that is to say when the COLOUR TEMPERATURE of the light source is around 6,500K. Daylight film is also suitable for use with electronic flash and blue flash bulbs.

Dedicated flash SEE FLASH

Definition
The sharpness of detail and general clarity of a photograph. Definition depends on several factors – accurate focusing, the quality and resolving power of the lens and the speed of the emulsion.

Defocusing
Technique of deliberately putting the image out of focus, which has the effect of spreading shapes and

softening colours. Best employed in simple shapes and silhouettes.

Density
The light-absorbing power of a photographic image, which varies in proportion to the deposits of metallic silver in an emulsion following exposure and DEVELOPMENT – in general terms, the opaqueness of a negative or the blackness of a print. Density can be measured by a special instrument called a DENSITOMETER; a logarithmic scale is used in measurement, 1.0 representing 100% absorption, and 0.3 representing 50% absorption. A graph of densitometer measurements plotted against a logarithm of exposures produces a CHARACTERISTIC CURVE.

Depth of field see page 48

Depth of focus
Very narrow zone on the image side of the lens within which slight variations in the position of the film will make no appreciable difference to the focusing of the image. As with depth of field, depth of focus increases as the

DEFOCUSING

DARK SLIDE

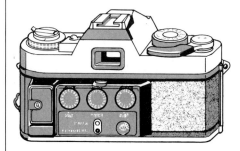

DATA BACK

Darkroom

Light-proof room used for processing and printing photographic materials, and where light-sensitive materials can be inspected under safelights.

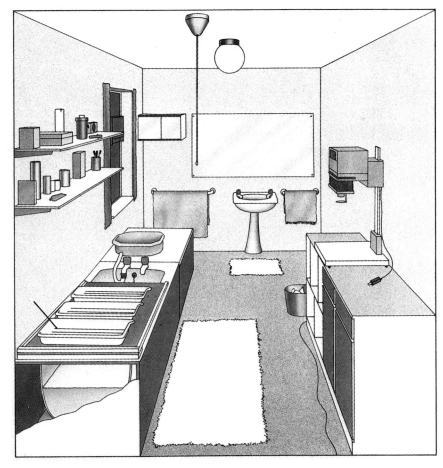

DARKROOM: Domestic bathrooms are particularly suitable for adaption as temporary darkroom because water and drainage is already available, and many bathrooms have a window small enough for blacking out. Processing trays can be sited on a work bench designed to fit on the bath, likewise the washing tank. If there's room, install a cupboard as an enlarging table and a storage for chemicals so that the bathroom can be easily restored to normal.

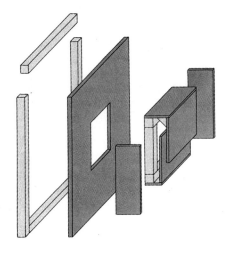

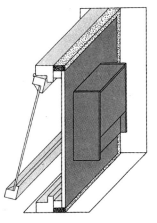

*Ventilation is necessary if a darkroom is used for any length of time. Cut a hole in the hardboard cover of a light, tight window frame (**above**). Behind this construct a double right-angled channel of wood.*

*To make a work surface (**right**) use blockboard rimmed with softwood. Drill holes in the board, and prop it at a slight angle so spilt chemicals can fall into the bath.*

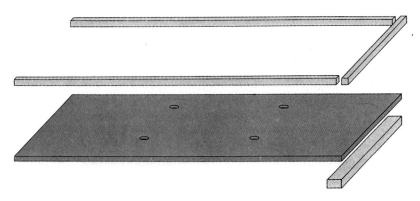

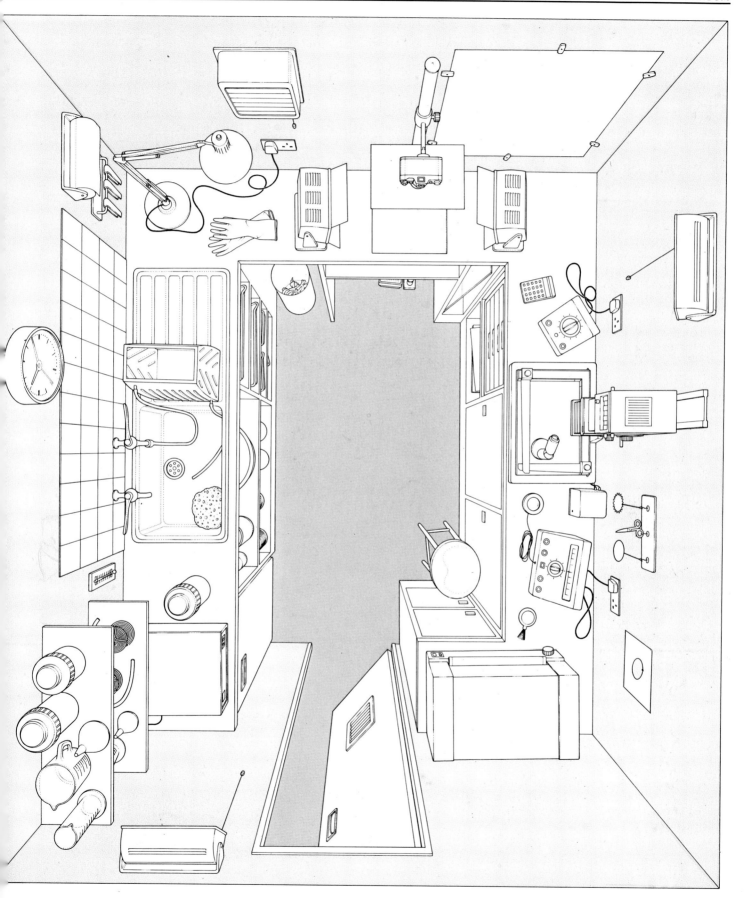

Depth of field

Zone of acceptable sharpness extending in front of and behind the point on the subject which is exactly focused by the lens. Depth of field varies with (1) the distance of the point focused from the lens (the shorter the distance, the more shallow the depth of field); (2) the size of the aperture (the smaller the aperture, the greater the depth of field); (3) the focal length of the lens (the greater the focal length, the shallower the depth of field). The zone of sharpness behind the point focused is greater than that in front of the point except in extreme close-ups, where there is approximately equal depth of field on either side of the plane of sharpest focus. Depth of field can be calculated in various ways, and most lenses have a depth of field scale inscribed on them. Many modern SLRs also have a depth of field preview button that closes the lens DIAPHRAGM to the f number selected and enables the depth of field to be assessed on the viewing screen. The drawback of this method is that the screen darkens progressively as the diaphragm is closed. Control of depth of field is one of the most useful weapons in the photographer's armoury, as the overall sharpness required in, say, an interior shot of a building might be quite inappropriate for a soft romantic portrait. Perhaps the most obvious and useful way of using restricted depth of field is the blurring out of unwanted backgrounds and foregrounds. When photographing animals through bars in a zoo, for example, at a suitable combination of aperture and distance, the bars can be made to disappear from the image so the subject is seen unimpeded.

Telephoto lenses have a very shallow depth of field, especially at wide apertures. At f/2.8 only the ball in front is sharp.

At f/5.6 depth of field begins to take in the middle distance.

DEPTH OF FIELD: *The three ways by which you can exploit and vary depth of field are 1) Aperture size – the narrower the aperture the greater the depth of field 2) The distance from your lens to the point focused on – the greater the distance, the more extensive the depth of field, 3) The focal length of your lens – the longer the length the shallower the dpeth of field.*

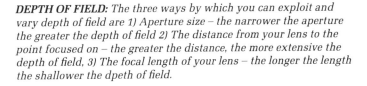

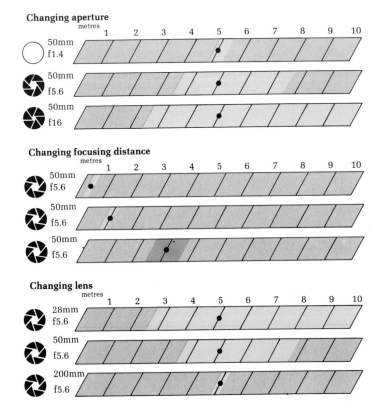

To get all the balls sharp, the lens needed to be stopped down to the smallest aperture at f/22.

With a standard
50mm lens at f/2.8
and focused on the
ball in the centre,
depth of field is
shallow.

At f/5.6 depth of field
begins to extend
behind and in front
of the central ball.

At f/22, the maximum
closed aperture,
depth of field, or zone
of sharpness, covers
all the balls on the
table.

A wide-angle lens
has a
characteristically
generous depth of
field, although at
f/2.8 there is a loss of
definition in the
foreground.

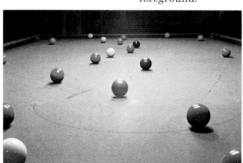

At f/5.6 depth of field
is good.

At f/22 there is
maximum depth of
field and a wide
angle of view.

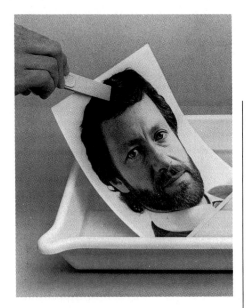

DEVELOPMENT

aperture is reduced, but the effects of subject distance and FOCAL LENGTH are opposite to those for depth of field; depth of focus increases the nearer the point focused is to the lens and the longer the focal length. Depth of focus also differs from depth of field in that the former is a concern of the camera designer and manufacturer rather than the camera user, dictating the degree of accuracy with which the film needs to be positioned.

Desensitizers
Chemical dyes that reduce the sensitivity of a film emulsion to light, allowing development by INSPECTION under a brighter light than usual. For example, a bright green safelight can be used to inspect fast PANCHROMATIC films. Desensitizers do not affect the latent image, but some types can affect the action of the developer. Typical dyes are the pinacryptols, employed as a forebath to treat the film prior to development.

Developer
Solution containing a number of CHEMICALS that convert the LATENT IMAGE in an exposed photographic material to a visible image. In addition to the developing agent that reduces the exposed halides to black metallic silver, the solution may also contain an ACCELERATOR, usually an ALKALI such

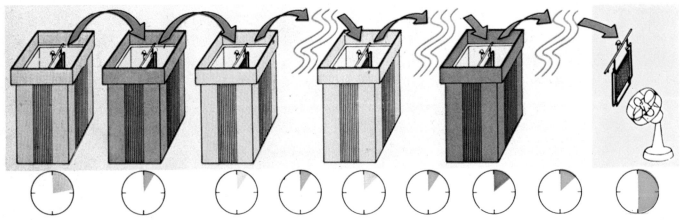

COLOUR NEGATIVE DEVELOPMENT

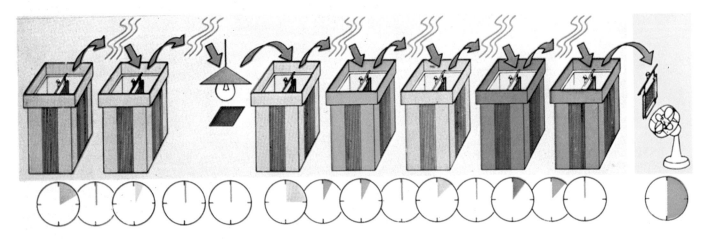

COLOUR TRANSPARENCY DEVELOPMENT

as sodium carbonate, sodium hydroxide or borax, which helps to speed up the action; a preservative, such as potassium metabisulphite, which helps to avoid stains and extends the life of the developer; and a restrainer, usually potassium bromide, which acts as an overall controller of chemical action, and also helps to reduce fog.

Developer improvers
Chemicals with anti-fog properties that can be added to conventional developers, or may already be included in the ingredients of a developer.

Development
The formation of the latent image into a visible image either by physical or chemical processes. Historically, developing processes were at first physical, i.e. the latent image attracts a deposit of metallic silver or, in the case of the DAGUERREOTYPE, mercury. A popular (though probably apochryphal) story relates that the discovery of photographic development by Daguerre was accidental: he left an exposed, iodized silver plate in a cupboard containing a quantity of mercury. On returning later to inspect the plate Daguerre was astonished to find that the previously plain surface now bore a picture. Vapour from the mercury had precipitated molecules of the metal on the invisible structure of the silver iodide to create a visible image. The mercury had an affinity with the silver and stuck to it like iron filings to a magnet. This is physical development or, rather, intensification, and occurs, for example, in the COLLODION PROCESS, where the developer, ferrous sulphate, causes precipitation of silver molecules on the latent image. Chemical development, on the other hand, converts the exposed SILVER HALIDES into metallic silver in presence of an ALKALI such as ammonia. The importance of alkaline development in creating a finer image

structure and rapid action was simultaneously and independently discovered by C. RUSSELL and Thomas Leahy in 1862.

Diaphragm
Part of the camera that determines the size of the APERTURE. The most common form today is the iris diaphragm. This is a system of overlapping metal blades forming a roughly circular opening that is continuously variable in size, adjustment being made by means of a ring on the lens barrel. The diaphragm can be placed in front of or behind the lens, but in compound lenses it is almost always placed between components. In a diaphragm shutter, the leaves can close completely in the centre, blocking out all light; diaphragm and shutter are thus combined in one mechanism.

Diapositive
Term that describes positive pictures on a transparent support, viewed by transmitted rather than reflected light. Colour transparencies and lantern slides are diapositives.

Dichroic fog
Processing fault characterized by a stain of reddish and greenish colours on the negative – hence the name 'dichroic' (literally 'two-coloured'). It is caused by the use of a contaminated or exhausted fixer whose acidity is insufficient to halt the development entirely. A fine deposit of silver is formed, appearing reddish by transmitted light and greenish by reflected light. The stain is difficult to remove, but in less severe cases can be treated with FARMER'S REDUCER.

Differential focusing
Technique of exploiting shallow DEPTH OF FIELD to make one part of a photographic image appear sharp while others are unsharp. It is a very useful device for blurring unwanted

DIFFERENTIAL FOCUSING (top and above)

elements or emphasizing the main subject, and can help to create a sense of depth or suggest atmosphere. Selective focusing is another commonly used term for the same technique.

Diffraction
Phenomenon occurring when light passes close to the edge of an opaque body or through a narrow aperture. The light is slightly deflected, setting up interference patterns that may sometimes be seen by the naked eye as fuzziness. The effect is occasionally noticeable in photography, as when, for example, a very small lens aperture is used.

Diffusion
Scattering of light when it is reflected from an uneven surface (diffuse reflection) or when it is transmitted through a translucent but not transparent medium. A reflecting surface does not have to be obviously rough, as even tiny irregularities (as in a layer of seemingly perfectly smooth paint) will scatter the light. The term diffuser, however, usually refers to a medium through which the light is transmitted (smoke or tracing paper, for example), rather than to a reflecting surface. Diffusion has the effect of softening light, eliminating glare and harsh shadows, and can therefore be a phenomenon of great value to the photographer. It is extensively used, for example in portrait photography (see BOUNCED FLASH and SOFT FOCUS). When coloured surfaces and media act as diffusers, some of the light is also absorbed.

DIN
Abbreviation for Deutsche Industrie Norm, used to designate one of the most commonly used rating systems for FILM SPEED.

Diopter
Unit of measurement of the strength of a lens, defined as the reciprocal of the focal length expressed in metres. It is most often used in photography to express the strength of a supplementary close-up lens or corrective viewfinder eyepiece on the camera.

Direct-vision finder
Any camera viewfinder (with or without optics) through which the subject is seen directly, rather than by reflection from a mirror. The advantages of a direct-vision finder over a reflex viewing system are that the subject can be viewed at the moment of exposure and that it is easier to see the subject clearly in dim lighting conditions. Disadvantages are PARALLAX ERROR and the fact that it is not possible to see the effects of, for example, filters or differential focusing before taking the photograph.

Disc camera
There are two types of disc camera: the still video camera in which the image is recorded on a magnetic disc and viewed on a television screen or print-out from a television set; and the Kodak disc camera aimed at the amateur photographer who seeks a compact, foolproof system at low cost. Kodak's camera is a slim ($\frac{3}{4}$in thick) fixed focus model taking discs of film each with 15 frames, yet permitting enlargement up to 10×8in. An integral motor rotates the disc and operates the exposure mechanism.

Dispersion
The splitting of lightwaves into visible component colours of the SPECTRUM when light passes through a refractive medium such as glass. The degree of dispersion depends on the angle of incidence of the light and the refractive index of the medium.

Dissolve unit
Device used in advanced slide projectors to alternately fade the images thrown by two projectors so

DISC CAMERA

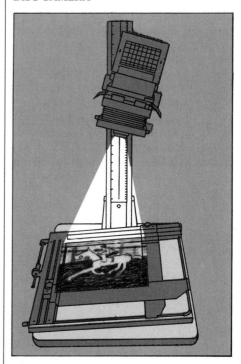

DISTORTION: Distortion of the image by tilting the enlarger head, or baseboard, can correct verticals, or create interesting effects.

DIFFUSION (far left)

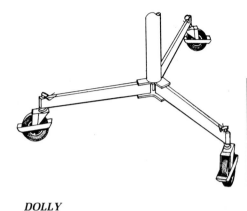

DOLLY

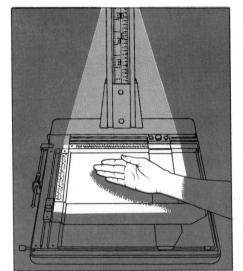

DROP FRONT

that there is a gentle transition between the successive images on screen.

Distortion

Alteration of normal shape or proportions within a photographic image, whether intentional, for expressive purposes, or accidental. Distortion can be produced by a variety of ways of altering the transmission or registration of the image, for example by using a lens very close to the subject or tilting the baseboard of the enlarger during exposure of the negative. ANAMORPHIC lenses produce one of the most spectacular types of distortion. Unintentional distortion is caused mainly by lens ABERRATION.

Diverging lens see LENS

D-max

Technical term for the maximum density which a given emulsion is capable of producing.

Dodging see also BURNING IN. Technique used in printing photographs when one area of the print requires less exposure than the rest. A piece of card mounted on a wire handle is held over the selected area to prevent it from receiving the full exposure. The 'dodger' (sometimes also called a 'paddle') is kept in constant movement to avoid abrupt changes in tone. The same technique using a hand instead of a piece of card is sometimes called shading, although many photographers make no distinction between the terms and use them interchangeably.

Dolly

Mobile support on wheels, used in the studio with large-format cameras and with lights.

Double exposure

Recording of two images on the same frame of film. It is a common method of achieving trick effects. Most cameras have some locking device to prevent making accidental double exposures. On older cameras it was often possible for this to happen if the photographer forgot to wind on the film after making an exposure.

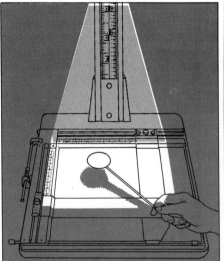

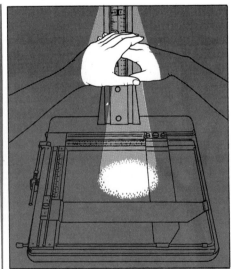

DODGING: *Edges of varied exposure can be blended by a rapid sideways hand movement.*

Tone can also be controlled by using a dodger or paddle.

A hole formed by your hands can concentrate a path of exposure.

Double extension
Characteristic feature of technical or similar cameras, permitting the lens to be moved up to two FOCAL LENGTHS from the film. This makes possible an image the same size as the subject.

Drift-by technique
Processing technique used to allow for the cooling of a chemical bath (normally the DEVELOPER) during the time it is in contact with the EMULSION. before use, the solution is warmed to a point slightly above the required temperature, but during processing it cools to a temperature slightly below, but still within, the margin of safety.

Drop front
Lens panel on some types of large-format cameras that allows the lens to be moved below the normal axis. It is one of the principal CAMERA MOVEMENTS.

Drying marks
Blemishes on the film resulting from uneven drying. They are virtually impossible to remove from the emulsion side of the material.

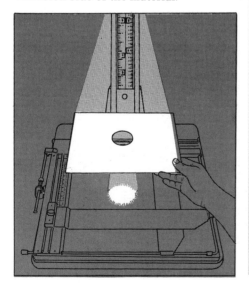

A square of card, with a suitable aperture, can perform a similar function.

DOUBLE EXPOSURE

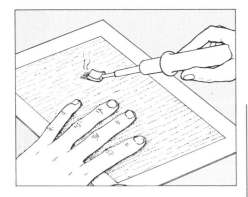

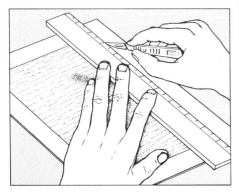

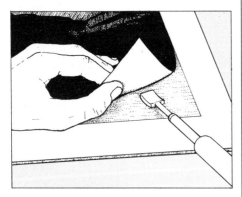

DRY MOUNTING

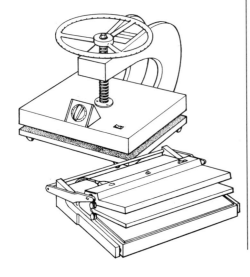

Dry mounting

Method of mounting prints on to card backing, using a special heat-sensitive adhesive tissue that is placed between the print and card and bonds them when they are placed in a hot press. It is the most effective method of mounting, as it produces a wrinkle-free and permanent result, and does not introduce any potentially harmful chemicals to the print, as do many glues.

Ducos du Hauron, Louis

French amateur photographer and scientist. With CHARLES CROS both independently published a SUBTRACTIVE system of colour photography, suggesting that pigments gave colour by subtraction, absorbing from white light all wavelengths save their own colour. This theory of colour reproduction was published by du Hauron as *Les Couleurs en Photographie, solution du probleme.* Du Hauron also outlined the principles of the additive synthesis, but in fact selected the wrong colours for the filters, mixing red, yellow and blue, instead of red, green and blue. Du Hauron's were the first successful colour photographs using his CARBON PROCESS where negatives through primary filters were turned into positives on gels containing carbon pigments in complementary colours. The inventive du Hauron also suggested the ADDITIVE method of stereoscopy and he patented a method of distorting images by using cross slits in place of a lens, which he called *'Transformisme en photographie.'*

Dupe

Abbreviated term for a duplicate slide.

DX coding

Kodak coding system, now employed by other film manufacturers, carried on 35mm cassettes and punched on the film itself, that conveys electrically a pattern of information to any camera designed to interpret the message. Cassettes marked with DX coding have 12 squares printed on the side in black and silver, and by varying the combination manufacturers are able to transmit such information as film speed, length of film, whether the film is slide or print, and so on. The film tongue, or leader, carries a punched hole 'raster' pattern that imparts information to the processing laboratory, and to the printer after the film has been processed.

Dye couplers

Chemicals used in colour film emulsions or in the processing developers that 'couple' with exposed silver halides to release dyes that form the colour image. The chemicals used in today's TRIPACK film to form subtractive dyes are commonly phenol for cyan dye development; pyrazolones for magenta; and acetoacetanilides for yellow. Couplers are complex structures, designed to form a molecular 'ball and chain' to prevent colour from wandering through the tripack layers.

Dye destruction process see also
CIBACHROME
Method of forming colour images by selectively eliminating dye by chemical means. It makes use of a tripack material that already contains the final dye in the emulsions before exposure. After exposure, a bleaching agent is used to destroy the dyes in proportion to the development of the silver halide image. Using this process it is possible to produce positive prints from colour transparencies without using an INTERNEGATIVE.

Dye sensitizing

The process of rendering A SILVER HALIDE emulsion sensitive to colours of light other than the blue to which the halides have an inherent response. The German chemist HERMAN VOGEL first carried out successful experiments in this field in the 1870s and 1880s, and his work led to the PANCHROMATIC materials used today.

Dye transfer process
Complex but versatile method of producing colour prints involving the making of three separate negatives, one for each primary colour, and the subsequent registration of a positive dye image from each.

Eastman, George
Founder of the Kodak company, inventor of the Kodak box camera and of roll film, and enthusiastic promoter of mass-market popular photography. He formed the Eastman Dry Plate Company in 1881 using plate coating machines which he had invented and patented in 1879. He used stripping film – gelatine emulsion on a paper backing which he patented in 1884. Eastman followed this in 1889 with nitro cellulose film coated with silicate of soda and a gelatin emulsion and wound on a spool inside a protective black paper. This film coincided with the launch of the famous Kodak No 1 camera and Eastman's slogan 'You press the button, we do the rest,' the rest being, of course, the processing of the film by the new firm 'KODAK' – a word devised by Eastman which, he said, could be easily remembered and used in any language.

Eberhard effect
Development phenomenon whereby very small areas of the image have a greater developed density than larger areas that have received the same degree of exposure. The Eberhard effect, named after the German physicist Gustav Eberhard, who first described it in 1926, is caused by the same kind of exhaustion and displacement of developing solution that brings about EDGE EFFECTS; when an area is sufficiently small (less than

about 1mm across) the distance from side to side is so slight that in effect the whole of the area reacts as an edge, and has no centre that remains unaffected.

Edge effects
Development phenomena characterized by increased CONTRAST at the boundaries of areas with markedly different densities. The effects are produced when developer becomes rapidly exhausted in heavily exposed areas, and fresher developer from the adjacent area moves across to replace it. Thus the edge of the heavily exposed area receives more development than the average for that area (the displaced fresh developer penetrating only slightly into the area), and the edge of the adjacent, lightly exposed area receives less development than the average for that area, some of its development potential having been lost to the edge of the heavily exposed area. The resulting increased sharpness is an effect that is sometimes sought after, and can be emphasized by using a developer that exhausts rapidly and by avoiding AGITATION.

Effective aperture see APERTURE

Effective f number
Value used instead of the normal f number in close-up photography when the increased lens–image distance makes extra exposure necessary. The effective f number is calculated by dividing lens–image distance by effective aperture (see APERTURE). The terms effective f number and effective aperture are often confused.

Ektachrome
Colour reversal film produced by Kodak, using E-6 processing. Ektachrome was introduced in 1946, and uses the technique of sandwiching the dye couplers in the tripack layers. The film is popular with professional

DUCOS DU HAURON, LOUIS: The 19th century French scientist was a pioneer of colour photography, producing colour landscapes as early as the 1870s.

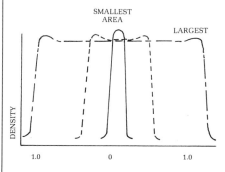

DISTANCE FROM THE CENTRE OF IMAGE (mm)

EBERHARD EFFECT

EKTAFLEX

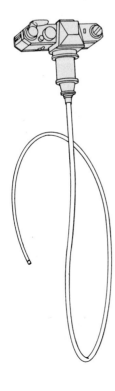

ENDOSCOPE

photographers since processing can be carried out by independent colour laboratories, thus processed slides can be returned in a few hours, or less.

Ektaflex

Kodak trade name for a dye diffusion colour printmaking system, radically simpler than the conventional procedure. It uses a special printmaker and chemical solution (activator), and instead of a single sheet of printing material, it uses two, both the size of the final print. The first, plastic-based, is exposed under the enlarger (there are two different types of material – one for working from negatives, one for working from transparencies), then soaked in the activator and sandwiched with the second, paper-based, sheet in the printmaker. After about eight minutes, the two sheets are peeled apart, revealing the finished paper print (either 7 × 5in or 10 × 8in). Much of the process can be carried out in daylight, and there is no need for washing and drying or for careful temperature control. These advantages of speed and simplicity are to some extent offset by the fact that the Ektaflex system is more expensive per print than conventional colour printing methods.

Electro-magnetic release

Shutter button that fires the SHUTTER through an electronic circuit in place of a mechanical system. Some cameras have both electronic and mechanical linkage.

Electronic flash see page 60 and also FLASH

Electron photomicrography

Production of photographs using an electron microscope, which is capable of higher magnification than conventional optical microscopes. In an electron microscope a high-velocity electron beam is emitted by a tungsten filament lamp, and the beam is conveyed through the specimen and on to a fluorescent screen by a number of magnetic coils, which bring the electrons to a focus much as a lens focuses light. The image produced by the electrons can be registered directly on to film. The film is mounted behind the screen, which is lifted when an exposure is to be made.

Emulsion

General term for the light-sensitive layer of films and printing papers. The conventional photographic emulsion is made up of ultra-fine grains of SILVER HALIDE suspended in gelatin. In most colour film, the sandwich, or tripack, of gelatin layers contains, in addition to the silver halides, COLOUR COUPLERS. Formerly, many other materials were used in the emulsion, some producing very distinctive effects. Platinum paper, for example, produced extraordinarily deep, velvety blacks, and the distinguished English photographer Frederick Evans was so devoted to it that he gave up photography when it became unobtainable during World War I. Some photographers (for example Irving Penn) make their own emulsions for specific purposes, especially printing papers, sometimes even using gold or platinum, and there has recently been a major revival of interest in old printing techniques using special papers.

Endoscopic photography

Technique of using an endoscope to photograph in small, confined areas inaccessible to a normal camera. An endoscope is an instrument consisting of a long tube containing optical and lighting equipment that relays the view seen from an aperture at one end of the tube to an aperture at the other, to which a camera can be attached by means of a special adapter. It was originally developed for use in medicine and this is still the major field in which endoscopic photography is used (enabling photographs to be taken inside the human body), but it is also employed in industry (photographing details of machinery, for example), and in other specialist areas such as photographing scale models. See also FIBRE OPTICS.

England, William

English commercial photographer, inventor of the focal plane shutter, founder of the London Stereoscopic Company, and enthusiastic stereo practitioner – he took the famous picture of tightrope-walker Blondin, balancing over Niagara Falls. England became a leading landscape photographer in the 1860s, using the recently introduced tannin collodion dry plate to shoot street scenes in London. The plates were convenient to carry around, but rather slow in sensitivity and recorded the moving figures and vehicles in the scenes as a blur – capturing movement on film was still beyond the scope of mid-19th century photographers. Given the limitations of the emulsion, England decided that a fast shutter was needed, with speeds well exceeding 1/60th second – the average 'fast' speed of the mid-19th century, and typical of the blind or drop shutters of the period. England devised a system where a roller blind with a narrow slit, set close to the film plane, passed across the film allowing the lens to perform at full aperture for the whole period of exposure. With this design, England invented the FOCAL PLANE SHUTTER now used – with variations – in all 35mm SLR cameras. Early focal plane shutters suffered from image distortion. As an authority at the time put it: 'If the shutter moves downwards, and a man is photographed as he is running, the man's head is first photographed, then gradually his body downwards, and then his legs. But he is moving, and therefore the lower part of the image may show him as if he were inclining backwards.'

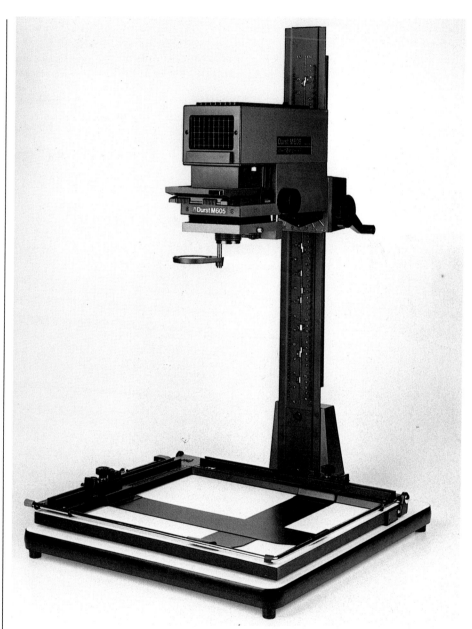

Enlarger see also CALLIER EFFECT and COLD CATHODE ENLARGER

Apparatus that makes enlarged positive prints by projecting and focusing the negative or transparency on to sensitized paper. There are two main types of enlarger available – those that use a condenser system and those that use a diffuser system.

ENLARGER: The major piece of equipment for the darkroom should be flexible enough to take several sizes of film stock, and suitably matched, good quality lenses and negative carriers. Most enlargers have a filter drawer for colour and black and white work, an alternative to the more versatile – and expensive – colour head.

Electronic flash

Artificial lighting in the form of a very bright, short-duration flash produced by a high-voltage electrical discharge between two electrodes in a gas-filled tube. The electrical discharge is activated when a circuit is closed by the camera's shutter SYNCHRONIZATION mechanism. Flash units are powered by dry-cell batteries, rechargeable cells or mains power.

Electronic tilt and swivel flashgun.

Studio flashlights fitted with diffusers.

KEYLITE

REAR OF KEYLITE

EVENLITE

SOFTLITE

SNOOT

BARN DOORS

Quad system: Electronic flash power unit which can be linked with up to three other units to increase output.

SLATS

HONEYCOMB

ENPRINT

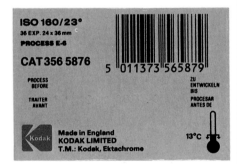

EXPIRY DATE

Enprint

Commercially produced fixed-ratio enlargement – usually $4\frac{1}{2} \times 3\frac{1}{2}$in from a 35mm negative.

Existing light

Alternative term (used chiefly in the USA) for AVAILABLE LIGHT.

Expiry or expiration date

Date marked on film packs to indicate the useful life of the emulsion. The date may be anything from 18 months after the time of manufacture for colour films to more than three years for black and white films. In practice, a film may stay usable well beyond the given date, especially if refrigerated, but the manufacturer's advice should generally be followed. As films age, the fog level rises, speed falls and colour balance changes.

Exposure

Total amount of light reaching the light-sensitive material during the formation of the LATENT IMAGE. The exposure is dependent on the brightness of the subject and the amount of light that is allowed to reach the light-sensitive material, the latter factor being controlled by APERTURE size and SHUTTER SPEED.

Exposure factor

Amount of increase in exposure required when using accessories such as bellows, extension tubes and filters, which extend the lens-to-film distance or reduce the intensity of the light reaching the film. It is usually expressed as a multiplication factor, and such factors are often marked on the rim of filters. A filter with an exposure factor (or filter factor, as it is often called in this case) of $\times 2$, for example, would require a doubling in exposure time or an increase in aperture size by one f number. Exposure factors are also occasionally expressed directly in stops.

Exposure latitude

Tolerance of a film emulsion to record satisfactorily if exposure is not exactly correct. Negative films generally have more latitude than reversal films.

Exposure meter see page 64

Exposure value

Numerical expression used to give a single value to the combined effect of APERTURE and SHUTTER speed on exposure. An exposure of 1/60 at f2, for example, is equivalent to one of 1/30 at f2.8 (twice the time at an aperture half the size), so they have the same exposure value. Exposure values are expressed on a logarithmic scale; the higher the exposure value, the smaller the amount of light admitted to the film.

Extension rings or tubes see page 66

F

Farmer, Howard see also CARBON
PROCESS
Ernest Howard Farmer, English
photographer and inventor of the
reducing bath (Farmer's Reducer),
which employs potassium ferricyanide
added to hypo, a method he published
in 1883. Farmer, who was the first
head of the Photographic Department
of the Regent Street Polytechnic in
London, also observed the action of
silver on BICHROMATED GELATIN. The
gelatin, in contact with a bromide
print, hardens without exposure
but in proportion to the density of
the silver image.

Farmer's reducer
Solution of potassium ferricyanide and
sodium thiosulphate, used to bleach
negatives and prints.

Ferrotype, or tintype
Cheap commercial process very
popular in the USA during the 1860s
and a derivation of the WET COLLODION
PROCESS. Ferrotype plates were made
of tinned iron, varnished black as a
backing for a collodion negative. The
process was invented by the French
amateur photographer Adolphe Martin
in 1853. Patents were taken out in
England, and in America, where the
process was also known as the tintype.
The ferrotype became very popular
with the itinerant street photographers
of the mid-19th century, since they
were simple to prepare, cheap to
produce and – unlike the
Daguerreotype and Ambrotype – very
robust. Later and more sophisticated
versions were devised, using dry
gelatin emulsions, designed for
automatic, on-the-spot processing of
plates: there were a few of these
machines at the turn of the century,
worked by an operator who provided
'while-you-wait' developing and
printing of your portrait.
    A process proposed by the
photographic scientist Robert Hunt in
1844 was also called ferrotype (not to

be confused with the above) and based
upon his discovery of ferrous sulphate
as a developing agent.

Fibre optics
Optical system that employs hair-thin
glass fibres to form 'light-guides'.
Fibres are coated with a material of a
low refractive index that effectively
traps light to contain it within the
length of the fibre; light entering at one
end is thus transmitted along the fibre
to emerge at the other end. The fibres,
or rods containing bundles of fibres,
will transmit light even when they are
bent or severely distorted, and can
therefore be used in the form of an
ENDOSCOPE to illuminate places
difficult of access, either for inspection
or photography.

Field See also COVERING POWER
The extent of the view or scene that a
lens is capable of conveying as an
acceptably sharp image. It can be
expressed as the angle that the
diameter of the maximum image circle
of acceptable quality subtends at the
lens.

Field camera see LARGE-FORMAT
CAMERA

Filament lamp see also FLUORESCENT
LAMP
Type of incandescent lamp in which
the light source is supplied by running
an electric current through a filament.
Filament lamps are a convenient
source or electric light for both
photography and domestic purposes.
In photography, TUNGSTEN FILAMENT
lamps are the most commonly used.

Fill-in lighting see page 68

Film
Sensitized material in the form of an
EMULSION coating a flexible base,
usually cellulose acetate or polyester.
The base is merely a support for the
emulsion: a film usually also has

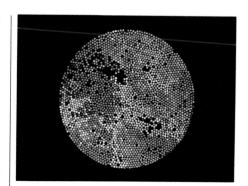
FIBRE OPTICS

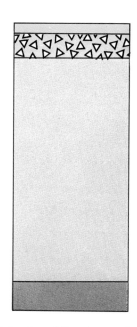
*FILM: Section of film shows gelatin
supercoat, emulsion, film base,
anti-halation backing.*

FILM DISC

Exposure meter

Instrument for measuring the intensity of light so as to determine the SHUTTER and APERTURE settings necessary to obtain correct exposure. Exposure meters may be built into the camera or be completely separate units. Separate meters may be able to measure the light falling on the subject (INCIDENT reading) as well as the light reflected by it (reflected reading); built-in meters measure only reflected light. Both types of meter may be capable of measuring light from a particular part of the subject (spot metering) as well as taking an overall reading. Built-in meters are often 'weighted' to a particular part of the image – most usually centre-weighted. The basic principle involved in exposure meters is that of light energizing a photosensitive cell to reduce the resistance to a flow of current that actuates a pointer or light emitting diodes (LEDs) indicating the light reading. LEDs are overtaking needles in popularity as they are easier to see in dim lighting and are more reliable, having no moving mechanical parts. Four main types of cell are used in exposure meters. (1) Selenium (Se): this type needs no battery power as it generates an electric current when exposed to light, but it is unsuitable for use inside a camera as it needs to be quite large to be sufficiently responsive in very dim conditions. (2) Cadmium sulphide (CdS): this like the two following types of cell, is small enough to be easily accommodated in a

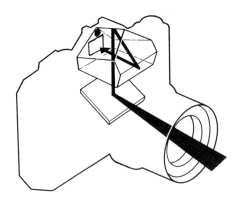

Pentaprism cell: In the most common system in SLR cameras, a sensor cell reads the light as it comes through the pentaprism and falls on the viewfinder screen.

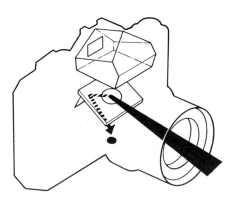

Transmitted light cell: System that takes the reading from light transmitted through a portion of the reflex via a second mirror to the cell. The mirrors flip up when the shutter is released.

camera, and like them is in circuit with a battery, the resistance of the cell changing in proportion to the intensity of the light. A cadmium sulphide cell has good responsiveness in dim light but a disadvantage is that it has a 'memory', which means it retains a reading for a few seconds, particularly with very bright scenes. This time lag can cause incorrect exposure in changeable lighting conditions, and CdS also has a tendency to underexpose red subjects as it is oversensitive to red light. (3) Silicon (silicon photodiode – SPD): this is also especially sensitive to red light and is often fitted during manufacture with a blue filter, when the cells are called silicon blue. The cells are fast-reacting

*SELENIUM METER
REFLECTED READING*

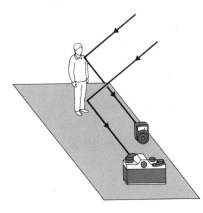

*CdS METER
INCIDENT READING*

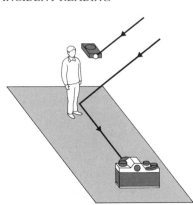

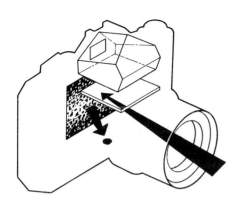

Off-the-film reading cell: Some sensors use transmitted light to give an approximate reading, later corrected to an accurate reading by metering light falling on the film, or a print-out on the shutter blind.

and have virtually no memory, but their reliability can suffer in temperature extremes. (4) Gallium arsenide phosphide (GaAsP or GPD): this is the newest type of metre cell and is fast-reacting and reliable. Built-in metres for SLR cameras are now almost without exception of the through-the-lens (TTL) type, which means that the reading is taken after the light has passed through the lens. TTL metering thus has the very great advantage of taking into account filters or any other lens attachments that modify the light reaching the film. In modern cameras the exposure meter is linked with the shutter and/or aperture diaphragm to give AUTOMATIC EXPOSURE.

SPOT METER
SPOT READING

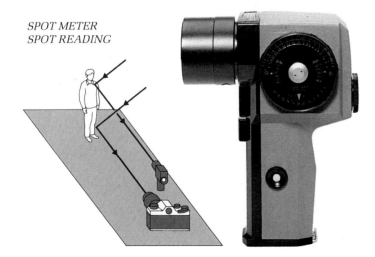

FLASH METER
FLASH READING

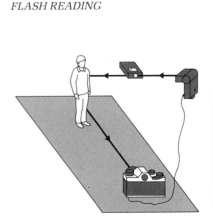

Extension tubes

Accessories used in close-up photography, consisting of metal tubes that can be fitted between the lens and the camera body, thus increasing the distance between the lens and the film. They are usually sold in sets of three, and can be used in combination with one another, making possible a variety of different extension lengths, and thus forming a serviceable, though less adaptable, alternative to extension bellows, which are continuously variable, but more cumbersome, ideally needing to be securely mounted. Extension rings may be automatic or non-automatic; the former, which carry the necessary mechanical linkage, allow open-aperture metering.

Fill in lighting

Additional lighting used to supplement the principal light source and lighten shadows. In portrait photography, for example, a single light source, such as available light streaming through a window, might cast very heavy shadows on one side of the sitter's face, and to achieve a better balance of contrast, an additional light, or the main light source 'bounced' off a reflector, would illuminate or fill in the shadow area.

*Some subjects need fill-in flash, or reflectors to balance contrast. For large interiors the method called "painting with light" can be employed, (**below**). The shutter remains open while the photographer moves around, firing off flash to make a combined exposure.*

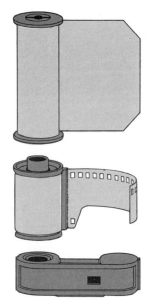

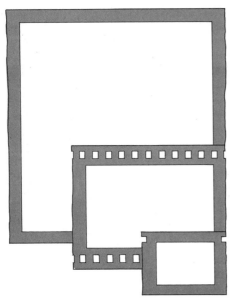

*FILM SIZES: Roll film (**top**), 35mm, and cartridge film*

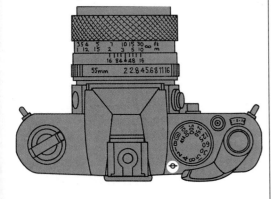

FILM PLANE INDEX

additional layers, the functions of which are to protect the emulsion. Black and white films generally have one layer of emulsion; tripack colour films, as the name suggests, have three layers in a sandwich or two sets of three layers. Colour negative film is used to produce prints, the colours of the subject being recorded in complementaries that are subsequently reversed again in the printing process to give the correct colours; colour reversal film produces a direct positive by effectively 'reversing' the negative image during processing. Films are manufactured in various types and sizes. Large-format cameras are loaded with single sheets of film, which come in sizes up to a normal maximum of 10 × 8in (25.4 × 20.3cm); other types of camera use film that comes in continuous strips, discs, or packs. There are five main methods of packaging film of this kind. (1) Cartridges: plastic containers that simply drop into the camera without any need for film threading. The film is wound from one side and stored in the other after exposure. Cartridges are made only in the smallest formats – 110 (13 × 17mm) and 126 (28 × 28mm) – and are used mainly in inexpensive viewfinder cameras. (The numbers used to designate film sizes – 110, 126, 135 and so on – are arbitrary, and have no relationship to one another.) (2) Cassettes: metal or plastic containers with a slit in the side that is lined with a velvet-like material to form a light-trap. A tongue of film protruding from the cassette is threaded on to a take-up spool in the camera, and when finished the film must be rewound into the cassette. Cassettes are used for 35mm film (36 × 24mm), and the widest variety of film types are manufactured in this form because of the popularity of the cameras (including most SLRs) in which this size of film is used. 35mm film can also be bought in bulk for loading into re-usable cassettes or special bulk film backs usually taking

250 exposures. (3) Roll-film: film wound on to spools and protected by a lightproof backing paper. It is used in medium-format cameras and is obtainable in a number of frame sizes, usually $2\frac{1}{4}$in (6cm) wide; 6 × 4.5 cm, 6 × 6cm, 6 × 7cm and 6 × 9cm are the most popular formats. Roll-film is also available without backing paper, this thinner form allowing more frames per roll. (4) Discs: circular platters of film which are used in simple snapshot 'DISC CAMERAS'. (5) Film packs, used almost exclusively for instant film, contain a number of individual sheets, interleaved with paper tabs. Pulling the tab after exposure draws the film sheet through a pair of rollers to initiate processing, and brings a new sheet of film into position behind the lens. Some instant cameras dispense with the paper tabs and advance film by motor-drive.

Film plane index
Symbol found on the top plate of many cameras indicating the plane that the film occupies within the body. It is used as a reference mark from which to measure distance when exact accuracy is necessary in close-up work.

Film speed
Degree of sensitivity, or 'speed', of an emulsion expressed numerically for the purpose of exposure calculation. In the past, numerous systems, both proprietary and national, have been used, among them H&D (Hurter and Driffield), Scheiner, Weston, BSI (British Standards Institution), DIN (Deutsche Industrie Norm), GOST (Gosudarstvenny Obshchesoyuzny Standart) and ASA (American Standards Association). GOST still has some currency in the USSR and Eastern Europe, but otherwise only ASA and DIN are now used, the former being an arithmetical system, the latter a logarithmic one. A film with a speed of ASA 200, for example, is twice as fast as one rated ASA 100; on the DIN

system the equivalent figures are 24°
and 21°, each increase of 3 indicating
that the sensitivity of the emulsion has
doubled. By recent international
agreement, these two systems have
now been incorporated in a new rating
system known as ISO (International
Standards Organization). Thus ASA
100 (21° DIN) now becomes ISO
100/21°.

Filter see page 72

Filter drawer

An adapter fitted to, or an integral part
of, a black and white enlarger for
colour work. The drawer holds filters
needed to produce the correct colour
balance. The sets usually contain
about seven filters of each of the
subtractive colours, cyan, magenta and
yellow, and covering a range of
densities. The enlarger should have an
infrared heat filter above the filter
drawer.

Filter factor see EXPOSURE FACTOR

Filter mount

Screw-thread in front of a lens to hold
filters, lens hoods, or other accessories.

Filter pack

Assembly of filters used in an enlarger
when making colour prints. Normally a
filter pack consists of any two of the
three subtractive primaries (yellow,
magenta, cyan) in the appropriate
strengths.

Fischer, Rudolph

German chemist and discoverer of the
principle of colour development.
Fischer investigated the chemical
construction of DYE COUPLERS that
linked dye molecules to developed
SILVER HALIDES in the image. The idea
that couplers could be used in the
subtractive TRIPACK had been
suggested by Carl Schinzel in 1905.
Fischer's discovery of 1912 was that
paraphenylendamine oxidized when
reducing silver halides to metallic

silver. The addition of reagents such as
the acetic esters produced a compound
of insoluble dye molecules, and these
formed only where the halides were
converted to black silver. By bleaching
out the silver image the subtractive dye
image remained. Fischer called the
process 'chromogene development'.
Unfortunately the new dye molecules
were inclined to migrate from layer to
layer through the tripack. The problem
was not solved until the 1930s, when
chemists at Agfa and Eastman Kodak
anchored the wandering dye couplers
by a chemical 'ball-and-chain' to larger
molecules.

FISCHER, RUDOLPH

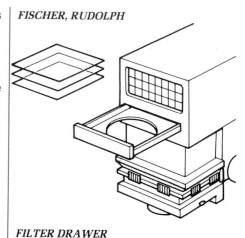

FILTER DRAWER

Filters 1

Sheet of glass, gelatin or plastic used to absorb or transmit a specific part of the light passing through it to alter tone or colour, or to manipulate the light to change or distort the image. Certain types or filter are employed in printing, but a much greater variety is used in front of the camera in both black and white and colour photography. In black and white photography a familiar example is the use of a yellow filter to darken the tone of the sky. Black and white film is particularly sensitive to blue lightwaves, and this means that in normal circumstances the sky areas of a negative are often overexposed and thus appear too pale on the resulting print. A yellow filter passes green and red light but absorbs light transmitted from the blue sky to give greater contrast between sky and clouds on the print. An orange filter will darken the sky still further. Filters used in such a way are called contrast filters, although, somewhat confusingly, the term correction filters is also sometimes applied to them. The latter term is best reserved for the colour conversion or correction filters (CC filters) used in colour photography to correct for small differences between the colour of the illumination used for

a particular exposure and that for which the film was manufactured, as when an amber filter enables tungsten film to be used in daylight. There are also colour filters used to actively change the colours of a subject; some do this so subtly that the fact that a filter has been used may not be apparent, and at the other extreme there are ones that completely transform the character of a scene.

Strong colour filters can produce startling results, but if they are not used with discretion the effects can be merely garish. A variety of special purpose and special effects filters is also available for colour and black and white photography. Of the former, the three most popular and useful are probably ultraviolet (UV) filters, neutral density filters and polarizing filters. A UV filter absorbs ultraviolet

radiation and helps to penetrate haze. As these filters have no effect on exposure they can be used to protect the lens from rain, dust and so on. (Skylight filters are very similar to UV filters, but they also absorb a small amount of blue light and thus have some of the effect of the contrast filters described above.) Neutral density filters are uniformly grey and reduce the brightness of an image without

*Threaded mount
filter for an SLR*

Filters 2

affecting either contrast or colour balance. They can be used to reduce depth of field (the reduction in the light reaching the film necessitating a larger aperture for a given shutter speed) and to enable fast films to be used in strong light beyond the camera's exposure controls. Polarizing filters cut down reflections from certain shiny surfaces. Special effects filters are of many different types. The most popular are probably starburst filters, which break point sources of light into dramatic star shapes, and multi-image filters, which produce repeated, overlapping images of the subject. Strictly speaking, these are not filters but optical lens attachments (just as polarizing 'filters' are more correctly called 'screens'); however, the usage of the word 'filter' to cover all attachments of this type is securely established. As with strong colour filters, special effects filters can produce extremely exciting results, but ones that through uninventive repetition can easily degenerate into photographic clichés. Filters are attached to the camera in either of two ways. Circular 'mounted' filters have metal rims that screw on to the lens, making different sizes of filter necessary for lenses of different diameter (the lens's 'filter size', expressed in millimetres). Square filters are slotted into a holder that can be fitted to lenses of various diameters by means of an adapter, so use of the filters is not confined to lenses of one particular size.

Polarizing filter

Cokin universal filter holder.

Kodak Porte-Filtre Professional No 2.

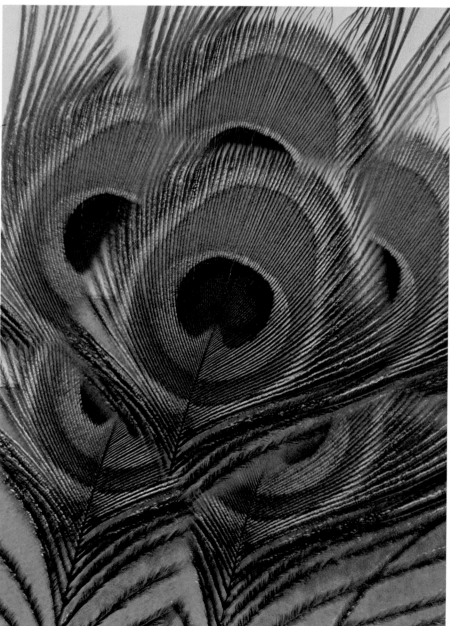

Star filters

Left: *multiple filter.*

Far left: *Graduated filter.*

Fisheye lens

Extreme wide-angle lens with an angle of view up to 180° or even beyond. Such lenses produce highly distorted circular images, cropped in all but the widest angle fisheyes to a square or rectangle by the film format. Straight lines passing through the middle of the picture appear straight on film, with the remainder of the image bowing outwards towards the edges, producing an effect similar to that seen in a distorting convex mirror. Focusing is usually unnecessary with fisheye lenses as they have enormous DEPTH OF FIELD. Fisheye attachments for standard lenses are cheaper than genuine fisheye lenses, but the quality of the results they produce is poorer and they usually demand a restricted aperture. A related device is the bird's-eye attachment, a clear tube that fits on the lens and by means of a spherical mirror in the tube creates a fisheye-type image looking behind the camera and in which the camera itself is seen.

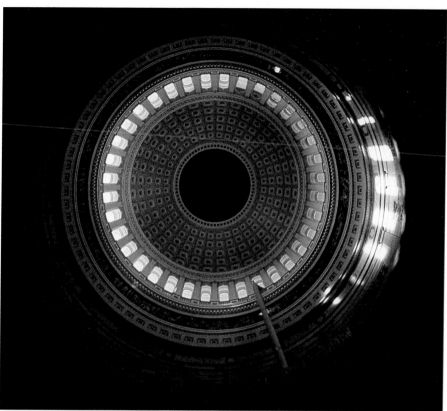

Standard lens (**above**) approximates the angle of view of the human eye. The fisheye (**right and below**) takes in a remarkable 180° view.

FLARE

FLASHING

Fixed focus lens

Lens focused at a fixed point, usually at the HYPERFOCAL DISTANCE. Most inexpensive cameras use this system, giving a focusing range from about 7 feet (2 metres) to infinity.

Fixer

Chemical bath needed to permanently establish the photographic image after it has been developed. The fixer stabilizes the emulsion by converting the undeveloped SILVER HALIDES into water-soluble compounds, which can then be dissolved out. Fixing agents belong to two main chemical groups: the thiosulphate group and the cyanide group. The latter are extremely rapid but highly poisonous and are thought to affect the permanence of the silver image. Sodium thiosulphate (hypo), first used by FOX TALBOT in 1841, still remains the most popular and the cheapest fixer.

Flare see also GHOST IMAGE

Light reflected within the lens barrel or between the elements of the lens, giving rise to irregular marks on the negative and/or an overall degradation of the quality of the image. Flare, which usually occurs when the camera is pointed towards a light source, is to some extent overcome by using COATED LENSES and having the interior surfaces of the camera treated with matt black paint and anti-reflection material.

Flash see page 80

Flashing

Printing technique in which the printing paper is given an auxiliary 'fogging' exposure by light that has not passed through the negative. The extra exposure may be spread equally over the whole print, reducing CONTRAST and producing a soft overall effect; it may be used for VIGNETTING so that the image merges into a black border; or it may be directed to a particular area by means of a torch to cause local darkening.

Floodlight

General term for an unfocused artificial light source that provides a constant and continuous output of light, suitable for studio photography or similar work. A floodlight usually consists of one or more tungsten filament lamps mounted in a reflector.

Fluorescence

Emission of radiation in the form of light from certain substances that have acquired energy from a bombarding source of radiation, usually ULTRA-VIOLET light. Substances that absorb light usually convert it into kinetic energy or heat, but fluorescent substances, which include many minerals, convert the short wavelengths of (invisible) UV light into longer wavelengths of (visible) fluorescent light. The fluorescence usually ceases when the source of energy is removed, but in some cases it continues – radiation of this kind is called phosphorescence. Fluorescent lamps consist of a tube internally coated with a fluorescing substance such as phosphor and containing mercury vapour, which produces UV radiation during an electric discharge. Fluorescent dyes are incorporated in the base of some printing papers to make white areas on the print appear more brilliant, especially when seen by daylight, which is rich in UV radiation. The phenomenon of fluorescence is also made use of in specialized branches of photography to create contrast that is not apparent in ordinary light. It is, for example, possible to detect falsifications to documents because of the different degrees of fluorescence of inks that might appear identical under normal lighting conditions. In such photography, a UV filter has to be used to prevent invisible radiation from reaching the film and thereby obscuring the effect caused by the fluorescent light.

F number see APERTURE

Focal length

Distance between the rear NODAL POINT of a lens and the point at which rays of light parallel to the optical AXIS are brought to focus when the lens is focused at infinity. The longer the focal length, the narrower the ANGLE OF VIEW of a lens.

Focal plane

Plane on which the image of a subject is brought to focus by a lens. In practical terms, the focal plane is the film itself.

Focal plane shutter see SHUTTER

Focal point

Point at which rays of light from a given object point meet after passing through a lens.

Focus finder

Small magnifying lens on a stand designed to assist focusing while making enlargements in the DARKROOM.

Focusing see also AUTOMATIC FOCUSING and DIFFERENTIAL FOCUSING

Adjusting the lens to film distance in order to form a sharp image of the subject on the film. On all but very simple cameras (which have a fixed lens operating at an aperture small enough to ensure that everything beyond a distance of a few feet is in focus) there is some means of changing the lens to film distance. On large-format cameras this is usually accomplished by moving the front (lens) panel relative to the back (film) panel to which it is joined by bellows; in smaller cameras the lens is usually adjusted with a screwing action. In large-format and reflex cameras the photographer can see on the FOCUSING SCREEN an exact image of what will be recorded on the film and can thus assess focus visually. In non-reflex cameras in which the image is not seen through the lens, focusing is done either by estimating the distance (basic cameras sometimes give a limited choice of settings related to symbols such as a head and a range of mountains for the shortest and longest distances) or in more sophisticated models by a rangefinder device. This works by comparing images of the subject reflected by two mirrors (or PRISMS) within the camera that move relative to one another as the lens is adjusted. When the images coincide (either two images overlapping perfectly or two halves of a split image joining) the subject shown is sharply focused. A split image device is also incorporated as a focusing aid in the focusing screen of many SLR cameras, which often have as an alternative or additional aid a system of MICROPRISMS that shimmer when the image is out of focus and become clear when it is sharp. Often the microprisms are arranged in a ring or collar around the split image device.

Focusing cloth

Small sheet of opaque cloth used to aid focusing with a large-format camera. It is draped between the focusing screen and the photographer's head and shoulders, cutting out external light from the viewing screen to enable as bright an image as possible to be formed on it.

Focusing hood

Folding hood incorporated in waist-level REFLEX CAMERAS as an aid to focusing. It surrounds the viewing screen, shielding it from light so that a clear, bright image can be seen. The hood often incorporates a magnifying glass that can be folded out for precise focusing of the central area. Some large-format cameras can take hoods that invert the image to appear upright.

Focusing screen

Screen of glass or plastic mounted in a camera to allow viewing and focusing

FLUORESCENT LIGHT

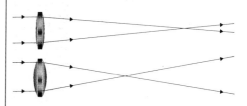

FOCAL LIGHT

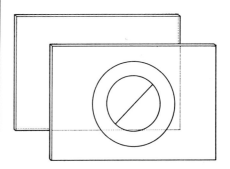

FOCUSING SCREEN

Flash

Artificial light source giving a powerful and very brief illumination, either by passing an electric discharge through a tube filled with an inert gas (electronic flash) or though an expendable flash bulb. Apart from packs of flashcubes such as Magicubes and Flashbars used on inexpensive and instant picture cameras, flash bulbs are now practically obsolete. Compact electronic flash units are built into many types of camera, but they have the disadvantage of a slow recycling period – a delay of more than ten seconds between shots is necessary for

1) Turn the calculator dial until the speed of the film in use appears in the window.

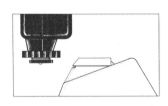

2) Slide the foot of the flash unit into the camera's hot shoe.

3) Set the shutter speed for flash, usually 1/60 or 1/125.

4) Gauge the distance to the subject. Then select the f stop (here f4 for 20 feet).

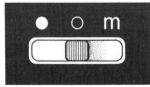

5) Slide power control to the setting that corresponds with the aperture chosen.

6) Switch on flash unit. You can take pictures when ready light glows.

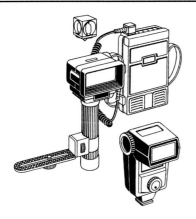

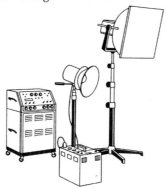

Umbrella reflectors can be used to reflect flash and give a soft light.

portraiture. In addition to the contact for flash on the hot shoe, many cameras have a socket to take an electrical lead so that flash can be used off-camera, enabling more varied lighting set-ups to be created. Flash is also used in the studio as an alternative to TUNGSTEN lighting. A disadvantage of flash is that it is not

the power to build up. Flashguns are lightweight units that can be mounted on the camera's HOT SHOE, and the majority are now "computerized", that is, they automatically adjust the duration of the light to the APERTURE setting, subject distance and film speed. The computer measures the strength of the light reflected from the subject and shuts off when a predetermined level has been reached – all, of course, in a tiny fraction of a second. Some computer flash units include a thyristor control (a solid state electronic switch), which conserves unspent energy and enables faster and more economical recycling. Many electronic flashguns have a tilt-twist head so that the flash can be bounced from a wall or ceiling (see BOUNCED FLASH), and some can be fitted with supplementary diffuser panels, filters and a means of spreading the beam of light for use with WIDE-ANGLE lenses. Dedicated flash units operate with only one make or model of camera, and automate most of the functions of the flash unit. All dedicated flash units set the camera's shutter to the correct SYNCHRONIZATION speed, and some also switch the camera back to "available light exposure" mode while the flash unit is recycling. Many dedicated units illuminate a READY LIGHT in the camera's viewfinder, and a few even measure flash exposure through the camera's lens, by means of a photocell which reads the light reflected from the film surface. Ring flash units are circular and fit around the lens. Ring flash casts no shadows, but produces an image that is soft and lacking contrast. It is used particularly in close-up work in medical or scientific photography and also in

possible to study the lighting effects of a set-up before the picture is taken, but it also has many advantages over tungsten lighting. Flash lamps are much cooler than tungsten lighting, and so are suitable for fragile subjects such as flowers or food and for portraits; they have a much longer life; their COLOUR TEMPERATURE is close to that of daylight, and so they can be used with daylight film; they provide very bright light and so can be used with small apertures to provide great DEPTH OF FIELD; and the brief duration of the flash they produce can be used to 'freeze' movement. In studio flash work, supplementary flash units can be triggered by a photoelectric device called a slave unit. This senses light from the main flash source and fires the secondary unit to which it is attached.

Ring flash, surrounding the lens, gives even frontal lighting without shadows.

FOX TALBOT, WILLIAM

FRESNEL LENS

of the image that the lens forms. GROUND GLASS focusing screens are used principally in large-format cameras. SLR cameras usually have a FRESNEL LENS incorporated in their focusing screens, together with one or more focusing aids, typically in the form of a MICROPRISM collar and/or a split image RANGEFINDER device. Some SLR cameras have interchangeable focusing screens suited to specialist subjects or the photographer's individual preferences. A screen with a grid of fine horizontal and vertical lines, for example, is a useful aid in architectural photography for ensuring correct alignment of the upright and transverse elements of buildings.

Fog

Veil of silver in a negative or print that is not part of the photographic image. Fogging is often accidental and can be caused in a variety of ways: optically, by stray light entering the camera or film cassette and exposing all or part of the film; chemically, by faulty processing solutions such as an overactive developer or a weak fixer containing heavy deposits of silver salts (see DICHROIC FOG). It can even be caused by vapours in the darkroom. Intentional fogging is a stage in the processing of colour reversal film. In those areas where unexposed and unwanted SILVER HALIDES remain on the developed image, they must first be chemically fogged and developed before being BLEACHED away.

Fog level

Density of fog produced when an unexposed film is developed. For a film to register an image properly, the minimum density produced by exposure must be above fog level.

Forced development see also PUSHED DEVELOPMENT

Development that is extended beyond the normal level to attempt to increase the density of an underexposed negative. It is used particularly when a film has been uprated. The price paid for the increased density is greater graininess and the risk of a high fog level.

Format

Dimensions of the image recorded on film by a given type of camera. The term may also refer to the dimensions of a print.

Fox Talbot, William

English inventor and mathematician, botanist and philologist, born at Lacock Abbey in Wiltshire in 1800. For his invention of the negative/positive photographic process, Fox Talbot is widely regarded as the 'father of modern photography', while his CALOTYPE PROCESS won him the medal of the Royal Society in 1842. Fox Talbot, Herschel, Daguerre, Niepce, Clerk Maxwell – these men were the founders of the basic photographic processes: Niepce for the first photograph ever recorded; Herschel for fixing the image; Daguerre for popularizing photography and for discovering development; Clerk Maxwell for the first photograph in colour; Fox Talbot for the negative/positive system – the basic method of reproducing multiple images from one original.

Frame counter
Indicator on a camera showing the number of frames already exposed.

French flag
Studio accessory used for shielding a lens from flare. Usually a black metal rectangle on a multi-jointed arm, clamped to a stand or the tripod.

Fresnel lens
Lens consisting of a plane surface on one side and a series of concentric stepped rings, each a section of a convex surface, on the other. This construction, in which the stepped rings collectively refract the light to the same extent as would a single more bulbous convex surface, produces a very flat lens of light weight which provides even illumination and sharpness all over, with no fall-off at the edges. Fresnel lenses are mainly used in spotlights and focusing screens.

Front projection
A means of projecting an image to provide a background to scenes shot in studios. The projector is set at right-angles to the camera and a background is projected on to a special high-gain screen via a semi-silvered mirror (through which the camera can see) set at 45° in front of the camera lens.

Front surface mirror
Mirror employed in reflex camera having a polished surface instead of a conventional mirror with a reflective backing. A front surface mirror eliminates the unwanted secondary reflection that is a characteristic of conventional mirrors.

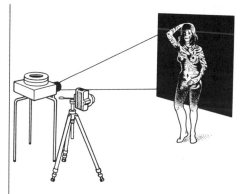

FRONT PROJECTION: *Front projection is used to provide a background to scenes shot in studios. With the exposure set for the image on the screen, the models are lit separately to match that exposure.*

G

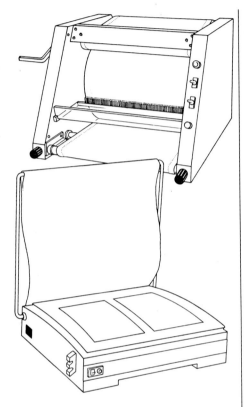

GLAZING

GLOSSY PAPER

Gabor, Dennis

Hungarian scientist and inventor of HOLOGRAPHY, which he described in 1948. In 1971 Gabor was awarded the Nobel Prize in physics.
Hungarian-born Gabor was an independent inventor, working in Britain while seeking a pure 'coherent' source of light to perfect his theory. The strongest light available to Gabor was a MERCURY VAPOUR LAMP, by which he was able to demonstrate that holography – the reproduction of images in three dimensions – was possible. With the invention of the LASER – an amplified beam of light with a regular frequency – Gabor's theory became an 'invention with a future'. The application of laser light to holography was the work of two American scientists, Emmett Leith and Juris Upatnieks, at the University of Michigan.

Gamma

Measure of the gradient of the straight line section of the CHARACTERISTIC CURVE, expressing the contrast of a given photographic material under specified conditions of development. On a characteristic curve graph the vertical axis represents density (D) and the horizontal axis represents the log of the exposure (E): gamma (γ) = D/log E.

Gamma rays

Rays emitted by radioactive bodies – similar to X-rays but of shorter wavelength and possessing greater powers of penetration. Gamma rays are used in industry to reveal and record on film the internal structure of materials in much the same way as X-rays are used in medicine to 'see' inside the human body.

Gel

Material, usually coloured plastic, that acts as a filter for a spotlight. The term is short for gelatin filter, although gelatin is now rarely used.

Gelatin

Substance used as the binding agent for the grains of silver halide in photographic emulsions. Gelatin, which is also used to make filters, is an animal protein, for which completely satisfactory synthetic alternatives have not been devised. The properties that make it especially suitable for use in emulsions are transparency, flexibility, permeability by the solutions used in processing, the ease with which it can be converted from liquid to solid, and its protective bonding action towards silver halide grains.

Ghost image

Image of a light source or bright highlight formed on the negative by unwanted reflections from the internal surfaces of the front and back elements of a compound lens. A ghost image, then, is a particular kind of FLARE, consisting of an identifiable image such as a light source, and can be largely overcome by using COATED LENSES.

Ghost photograph

One of the commonest types of trick photograph, produced by double exposure. Two exposures of the same scene are made on a single sheet or frame of film, identical except that in the second a figure is introduced. In the resulting print the figure appears as a transparent ghostly presence.

Glazing

Process by which glossy prints can be given a shiny finish by being dried in contact with a hot drum or metal sheet of chromium or steel plate.

Glossy paper

Printing paper with a smooth and shiny surface. Glossy paper produces sharp prints with deep blacks, bright highlights and clear detail, and is therefore much used for technical photographs and those intended for reproduction. A drawback of glossy paper is that it tends to show up blemishes much more clearly than textured or matt surfaces, where the greater scattering of light (see DIFFUSION) makes faults less noticeable. For the same reason it is more difficult to retouch glossy prints.

Goldberg wedge
Wedge-shaped layer of tinted GELATIN sandwiched between glass, used in sensitometry. The density of the gelatin increases in measurable degrees from the thin to the thick end of the wedge, and negative densities can be compared with these known values.

GOST
Abbreviation for Gosudarstvenny Obshchesoyuzny Standart (Soviet Government All Union Standard), used to designate a rating system for FILM SPEED used in the USSR and some Eastern European countries. GOST is a mathematical system similar to ASA.

Gradation
Term used to describe the range of contrast or tonal variation in a photographic image. An image that has many different intermediate tones between the darkest and lightest parts is described as having a soft gradation; when there are few variations between light and dark, the image is said to have a hard gradation. Gradation depends initially on the speed of the film, slow film producing hard gradation and fast film soft gradation, but it is also affected by DEVELOPMENT. Concentrated and extended development leads to hard gradation, dilute and shortened development to soft gradation.

Grade
Term used to describe the degree of CONTRAST of black and white printing papers. They are usually available in a variety of different grades, although with MULTIGRADE PAPER the contrast is controlled by means of filters.

Grain
Granular texture appearing to some degree in all processed photographic materials. In black and white photographs, the grains are minute particles of black metallic silver that constitute the image. In colour photographs, the silver has been removed chemically, but tiny blotches of dye retain the appearance of graininess. The faster the film, the coarser the texture of the grain. Grain may be undesirable in photographs that aim to convey maximum sharpness and detail, but it can also produce arresting pictorial effects that are appropriate for the subject, conveying intimacy, for example, in candid shots. The term granularity is applied to the objective measurement of grain, the term graininess to its subjective assessment.

Grey card
Card of a standard reflectance, used to obtain average reflected light exposure readings.

Grey scale
Series of grey tones arranged (on a print or transparency) in a regular order of increasing or decreasing depth of tone, used as a standard against which measurements can be made in sensitometry.

Ground glass
Translucent glass with a granular textured surface on one side on which images can be formed. It is used primarily in focusing screens.

Guide number
Indication of the power of a flash unit, expressed in feet or metres, enabling the correct aperture to be selected at a given distance between flash and subject. The number divided by the distance gives the f stop to be used. A film speed is specified with the guide number, and a new guide number is needed for different speeds.

GRAIN

GREY SCALE

HALATION: A diffused image, formed around the image of a bright light source, occurs mainly in night photographs.

Halation
Phenomenon characterized by a halo-like band around the developed image of a bright light source. It is caused by the internal reflection of light from the support of the emulsion – the paper of the print, or the base layer of a film. While technically it may be considered a fault (negative materials usually have an ANTI-HALATION backing to prevent it), the phenomenon can create interesting effects of light, and in some pictures may be considered an advantage.

Half-frame
Film format measuring 24 × 18mm, half the size of the standard 35mm frame.

Half-plate
Term used to describe a negative or (now more commonly) a print measuring $4\frac{1}{4} \times 6\frac{1}{2}$ in.

Halogens
Group of chemical elements, among which chlorine, bromine and iodine are included. These elements are important in photography because their compounds with silver (SILVER HALIDES) form the light-sensitive substances in all photographic materials.

Hardener
Chemical used to strengthen the gelatin of an emulsion against physical damage caused, for example, by scratches on the surface and high temperatures in processing and drying.

Hauron, Ducos du see DUCOS

Heat filter
Device that absorbs heat radiation from a beam of light without affecting its degree of illumination. Heat filters are used mainly in projectors and in some enlargers.

Hellot, Jean
Eighteenth-century scientist whose 'invisible writing' is the first recorded experiment with silver nitrate on paper. Using a diluted solution of silver nitrate Hellot showed how his magic 'ink' became visible when exposed to strong sunlight, which Hellot wrongly assumed was caused by sulphur in the nitric acid. He described his silver ink as '*Une Nouvelle encre sympathique.*'

Helmholz, Herman von
German scientist who in 1852 discovered the theories of colour proposed by THOMAS YOUNG in 1801. Helmholz reviewed Young's work and made his own contributions, and published in 1888 the 'Young-Helmholz' theory of colour vision.

Herschel, Sir John Frederick William
Probably the most inventive of all early pioneers of photography. In addition to being the first to discover sodium ferrosulphate as a fixing agent, he made photographs independently of DAGUERRE and FOX TALBOT, using silver carbonate on paper. He was the first to use the terms 'negative' and 'positive'. He invented a process for obtaining direct positives on paper; he introduced photographs made on glass and with black backgrounds like the later AMBROTYPE; he discovered the highly sensitive properties of silver bromide, and actually obtained in 1839 – 20 years in advance of CLERK MAXWELL – a colour photograph of the spectrum. It is possible that Herschel, a man of genius, might have advanced the progress of photography by fifty years had he devoted himself solely to the subject. Such was Herschel's reputation that he was credited where credit was not entirely due: the first use of the term 'photography' is now ascribed not to Herschel, but to the German astronomer Mädler.

High-contrast developers
Developers based on hydroquinone

and alkali that yield very high-contrast results, especially with lith films, half-tone, document and line images.

High-key see KEY

Highlights
Bright parts of the subject that appear as the densest areas on the negative and as the lightest areas in prints or transparencies.

High-speed camera
A camera designed to make a number of exposures in extremely rapid succession for the study of short-lived phenomena. Some such cameras contain large quantities of film, and in principle resemble turbocharged cine cameras. Others, though, may make just a handful of exposures at precisely the right moment. Most high-speed cameras are used for scientific purposes and are highly specialized, but there is occasional news use of the less esoteric cameras – to photograph the launch of a spacecraft, for example.

High-speed processing
Method of rapid developing and fixing of photographic materials when conventional processing techniques are too slow. Picture editors of newspapers and agencies, for example, often need prints very quickly, and darkroom technicians use a variety of means to provide almost instantaneous (yet good-quality) negatives and prints. Some make up their own solution of such developers as Ilford's liquid Autophen (a Phenidone developer used in machine processors), ID 11 or microphen, warmed to just below the point where chemical fog might be a hazard. Negatives can be developed in 20 seconds, fixed in a minute with a rapid fixer, and dried in two minutes, the entire process taking less than five minutes. MONOBATH developers, which also incorporate a fixing agent, can develop and fix a film in three minutes.

Prints from these, though, may lack contrast, and there is a slight chemical fog, so the process has yet to be refined for commercial application.

Holography
Technique whereby information is recorded on a photographic plate as an interference pattern that, when viewed under the appropriate conditions, yields a three-dimensional image. Holography bears little relation to conventional photography except in its use of a light-sensitive film.

Homolka, Benno
German chemist working at the Farberwerke Hoechst who discovered the red dye and sensitizer Pinacyanol, and the densitizer Pinacryptol Green. Pinacyanol, discovered in 1904, led to development and production of the PANCHROMATIC plate, first marketed by the plate-making firm of WRATTEN AND WAINWRIGHT in Croydon.

HIGHLIGHTS: Two prints of a shot of eggs – the darker the print, the more prominent the highlights as contrast increases.

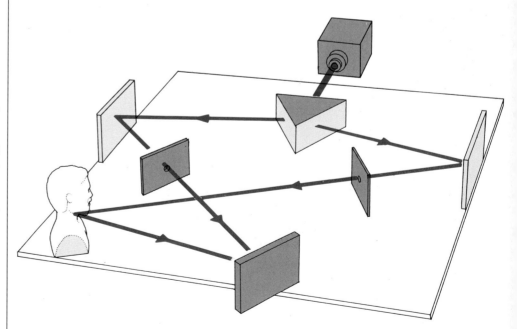

HOLOGRAPHY: Essential to the hologram is the beam of coherent white light (laser).

IMAGE FALL-OFF: Lack of definition that increases towards the edges of the picture. It can occur at wide apertures, especially with lenses of limited covering power.

HYPERFOCAL DISTANCE: sacrifices a sharp horizon, or infinity, by putting emphasis on a sharp foreground. At f/22, the entire picture is acceptably sharp.

Hot shoe
Fitting on top of a camera that incorporates a live contact for firing a flashgun, thus eliminating the need for a separate socket. It makes contact between the flashgun and the shutter circuit to provide flash SYNCHRONIZATION.

Hue
The title of a colour, the property that distinguishes blue, for example, from red. Hue is determined by wavelength; red has a longer wavelength than blue.

Hurter and Driffield
Pioneers of sensitometry and the creators of photographic photometry. Ferdinand Hurter and Vero Driffield invented in 1890 a system determining the speed and sensitivity of photographic emulsions. Both were amateur photographers, Hurter was a chemist by trade, and Driffield an engineer, and Hurter in particular became impatient with the then rule-of-thumb methods of exposure. They began to investigate a practical means of standardizing exposures to obtain what they termed a 'perfect negative,' one which reproduced all the tones of the subject, and in their proper proportions, regardless of the contrast. Using a candle to represent a standard illumination, they exposed a photographic plate in sections at exposures rated from 2.5 through to 320 candle meter seconds, but leaving one part of the plate unexposed. After processing, the sections were measured from the unexposed 'fog level' through the threshold exposure plotting a logarithmic curve of densities on a graph. This 'CHARACTERISTIC CURVE' of net densities gave Hurter and Driffield their 'H & D Numbers', which were directly proportional to the speed of the plate. The two researchers, over a period of several years, determined the effects of sunlight on photographic materials at different times of the day, and through the year, noting the effects of the weather. These calculations, added to those of their other experiments, gave Hurter and Driffield the basis for their Actinograph exposure meter of 1888.

Hyperfocal distance
The shortest distance at which a lens can be focused to give a depth of field extending to infinity. Depth of field extends in front of the focused point as well as behind it and when the lens is focused on the hyperfocal distance, depth of field will in fact extend from half that distance to infinity.

Hypersensitizing
Term used to describe any method of increasing the speed, or sensitivity, of a photographic emulsion after manufacturing and before exposure in the camera; treatment after exposure is known as LATENSIFICATION.

Hypo
Colloquial name for sodium thiosulphate, which until recently was used universally as a fixing agent. The term was thus once generally used as a synonym for FIXER.

Hypo eliminator
Solution for removing traces of hypo from negatives or prints so as to reduce washing time. It is used particularly in HIGH-SPEED PROCESSING.

Illuminance see also LIGHT UNITS
The measure of the strength of light.

Image
Optical representation of an object or subject formed by rays of light reflected or refracted from it. An image formed on a physical surface (such as a focusing screen) is called a REAL IMAGE. When such an image is formed on a plane in space rather than on a surface, it is called an aerial image. An image which cannot be formed on a screen is called a virtual image. Such an image (for example, that which we see in a mirror) is seen in a position through which rays of light appear to have passed, but have not. The invisible image formed during exposure is called the LATENT IMAGE.

Image fall-off see ABERRATION, COSINE LAW and COVERING POWER
Deterioration of definition and/or brightness towards the edges of an image formed by a lens.

Image intensifier
Electronic device placed between the lens and camera body to increase image brightness. Essentially, the device consists of an evacuated glass envelope with a semi-transparent photo-cathode at one end and a television-type luminescent screen at the other. The photo-cathode receives the image and emits a pattern of electrons proportional to the brightness of the image which the screen then converts back into visible light. Image intensifiers can be used only for black and white photography.

Image plane
Alternative term for FOCAL PLANE

Imbibition print see CARBON PRINTING

Incident light
Light that falls on a subject or surface as distinct from light that is reflected from it. Many hand-held exposure

meters are able to measure the incident light in addition to the reflected light.

Indicator
Chemical or chemicals that when added to a processing bath indicate certain features about its condition, particularly the pH factor (degree of acidity or alkalinity), which shows the effectiveness of the solution.

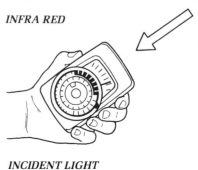

INFRA RED

INCIDENT LIGHT

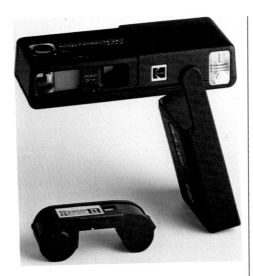

INSTAMATIC CAMERA

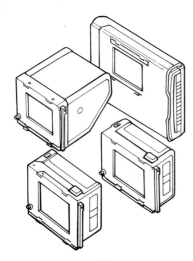

INTERCHANGEABLE BACK: Medium format cameras with interchangeable magazines enable you to quickly switch from one format to another. Particularly useful to professional photographers is the polaroid back by which exposure, composition and other factors can be judged before the final shot on negative or slide film.

Infinity

Theoretically, a point which is immeasurably distant; in practice, a point at such a distance from the camera that moving beyond it makes no difference to the sharpness of the image focused by the lens. The infinity setting, marked on the camera by the symbol ∞, places the lens one FOCAL LENGTH from the film plane, giving a sharp image of distant objects.

Infrared

Radiation with a WAVELENGTH longer than that of visible red light. Infrared radiation may be felt as heat, and can be recorded on suitable types of photographic film. Special dyes within its emulsion make infrared black and white film sensitive to these long wavelengths. Surfaces that emit infrared radiation appear as white on the finished print, other surfaces appearing as black. Deciduous foliage, for example, reflects infrared, creating the ghostly effect of white trees against a black sky. Infrared colour film is a tripack reversal film sensitized to green and red, but with the blue-sensitized layer replaced by one that is infrared sensitive. Infrared colour film produces an image that is predominantly magenta-coloured, but this can be altered by the use of filters. A green filter, for example, will change reds to orange, skin tones to yellow, and white to green. As well as producing such interesting effects, infrared photography has many specialist applications in various technical and scientific fields from plant pathology to the investigation of altered or forged documents.

Inspection development see also
DESENSITIZER
Brief inspection of the progress of image development on film during the processing. This may be done by holding the material against a suitable weak SAFELIGHT without fogging the image.

Instamatic camera

Simple fixed focus 126 format viewfinder camera, popularized as the 'Kodak Instamatic' and following the tradition of the famous Kodak 'BROWNIE'.

Integral tripack

Composite photographic emulsion used in virtually all colour films and papers, in the form of a multi-layer 'sandwich' of subtractive colour dyes coupled to silver halides. The layers are blue-sensitive for the yellow dye image; green-sensitive for the magenta dye; red-sensitive for the cyan dye. In addition to these three main layers, the emulsion contains other layers, such as a yellow filter to prevent blue light penetrating the red and green layers and an ANTI-HALATION layer. Including the film base, some colour print films have as many as ten layers.

Intensification

Technique of increasing the image density of a thin black and white negative, either with a chemical or dye intensifer, or by optical means. The chemical process is the one most widely employed, the negative being treated by immersion in chemical baths containing chromium, mercury or silver compounds that increase the size of the SILVER HALIDE grains. This will, of course, intensify only areas where halides exist, thus increasing the image contrast. Silver areas of the image can also be treated with dye toners, increasing the opacity of the negative and thus partially stopping the lightwaves passing from the enlarger to the print. Optical treatment by IRRADIATION consists of photographing the negative by a raking side light. The silver grains scatter the light within the emulsion, thus producing a denser image.

Interchangeable backs

Camera magazines designed to fit medium format cameras, each back taking a specific film size, varying through such formats as 120 roll film; 220 roll film; 35mm film, and polaroid Land film packs.

Interference

Alteration of the wavelength of light resulting from the meeting of two wavefronts, as when light reflected from the back of a thin film meets light reaching the front (see LIPPMAN PROCESS).

Intermittency effect

Phenomenon observed when an emulsion is given a series of very brief exposures, resulting in an image of weak density and loss of CONTRAST. The density of the image produced is lower than that produced by a single exposure of duration equal to the total of the short series of exposures.

Internegative film

Special type of film designed to produce copy negatives. It has a built-in mask against loss of SATURATION and against an increase in contrast inherent in the copying technique. Colour internegative film is often used to produce an intermediate negative from a colour transparency from which colour prints are required.

Intervalometer

Device that can be fitted to an autowinder or motor-drive to provide a predetermined delay between exposures in any one sequence. The delay may be variable from as little as a second up to several days.

Invercone

Attachable diffuser used with Weston exposure meters to make INCIDENT LIGHT readings. The diffuser is positioned over the cell window so that the meter measures the light falling on the subject from all directions. This method of taking an exposure meter reading discounts the reflectivity of the subject.

Inverse square law

Mathematical formula used in calculating the increase or decrease in light intensity falling on a surface as the distance between the surface and a point source of light changes. This change of intensity is calculated by inversely squaring the change of distance. At twice the distance the light has one-quarter the intensity. If the distance is reduced three times the intensity is increased nine times. The law applies only to light radiating from a single point source, and is used to calculate the guide number (flash factor) of flash bulbs and electronic flash.

Inverted telephoto

Short focal length lens with a comparatively long BACK FOCUS. Many WIDE-ANGLE lenses for 35mm cameras are of this construction.

Iris diaphragm see DIAPHRAGM

Irradiation

Scattering of light within the emulsion, caused by multiple reflections from the minute silver halide crystals. It increases the effects of HALATION, and is more prevalent in thick emulsions than in thin ones. Effects of irradiation can be partially controlled by using a high-actuance surface developer that speeds up the development of low-density areas adjacent to the areas of high-density irradiation.

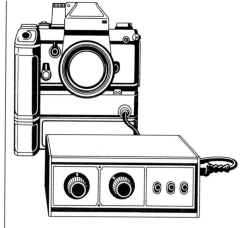

INTERVALOMETER

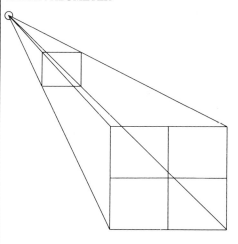

INVERSE SQUARE LAW

INVERTED TELEPHOTO

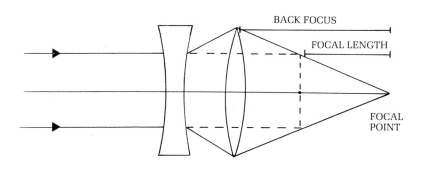

BACK FOCUS

FOCAL LENGTH

FOCAL POINT

J

IR setting

Mark sometimes found on the focusing ring of a camera lens indicating the shift in focus needed for INFRARED photography. Infrared radiation is refracted less than visible light, and the infrared image is therefore focused slightly behind the visible image.

ISO speed see FILM SPEED

Ives, Frederick

American photographer and inventor of many colour processes, and also inventor of the half-tone printing process. He devised several colour camera and colour image viewing systems based on the ADDITIVE SYNTHESIS, notably his 'CHROMOGRAPHOSCOPE', his 'Photochromoscope' of 1895, his 'Kromscop' lantern of 1895, and he also invented a 3-D cine camera.

IVES, FREDERICK

Joly, John

Dublin professor and inventor of the first linear screen colour plate to be introduced commercially. Joly's technique was to coat a glass plate with GELATIN, which when dried was superimposed with a series of very fine lines ruled across the gelatin with dyed gum, in red-orange, blue-green, and blue-violet colours. An advertisement of 1899 described the process: 'A negative is taken through a screen ruled with fine lines representing the three primary colours of the SPECTRUM. From this a positive is printed, which is mounted in contact with a similar ruled screen. The result is a reproduction of the object photographed, rendering, not only every detail of form and light and shade, but the most subtle play of colour, with a degree of exactitude and realism which can only be described as *startling*!' In fact, Joly's plates were not entirely successful because the orthochromatic plates of the 19th century were insensitive to red but highly sensitive to blue, and partial correction was required through a yellow filter. But success was just around the corner for the screen plate, when the LUMIÈRE BROTHERS. used the panchromatic emulsions introduced in 1906 in their AUTOCHROME plates.

Jos-Pé process

Colour printing process introduced in 1924, based upon the CARBON imbibition technique using additive colour separation negatives, made in the Jos-Pé camera. Named after its inventor, Jos. P. Welker, the camera had a beam-splitting system of PRISMS which transmitted light, via three mirrors, on to three separate plates through additive colour filters.

Joule

Unit of energy equal to one watt-second. In photography, the joule is sometimes used to indicate the output from an electronic flash.

Kelvin scale see COLOUR TEMPERATURE

Kennett, Richard

English amateur photographer, inventor of the first commercial dried gelatin emulsion, marketed as 'Kennett's Patented Sensitized Pellicle.' The product was also described as a 'washed' pellicle because Kennett had improved upon BURGESS's emulsion by washing out the crystalline salts formed by the interaction of bromide and silver nitrate, and visible in the negative. Photographers bought the pellicle, reconstituted it with water, heated the softened gelatin to make a pourable emulsion (often in a teapot, a handy darkroom accessory) and spread a thin film over a glass plate. Kennett claimed that his pellicle was 'the most sensitive plate ever brought before the public'. This was true, and the extra speed was due to the ripening of the emulsion in the heating and drying process (see BENNETT, CHARLES). Many photographers regarded the plates with some scepticism, and some refused to try them at all, preferring the much slower wet plates of the period. Used to long exposure times, photographers tended to overexpose the plates, either in the camera, or by the too-bright darkroom lamps that were suitable for only the slow wet plate. Kennett also produced ready-made dry plates, sold from his Maddox Street shop in London, but was obliged to reduce the speed of the emulsion when poor public response threatened his business.

Key

Term describing the prevailing tone of a black and white or colour photograph. 'High-key' refers to a predominantly light image; 'low-key' refers to a predominantly dark one.

Key light

The main source of light in any lighting set-up, determining the overall character of the illumination.

Kodak

The name given by GEORGE EASTMAN to his new camera of 1888, the 'Kodak' No 1, and also to the Kodak system of photography. 'It is now easy,' wrote Eastman, 'for any person of ordinary intelligence to learn to take good photographs in *ten minutes*.' All one had to do, said Eastman, was 'pull the string' (to set the shutter); 'turn the key' (to wind on the film); 'press the button' (to fire the shutter).

The name Kodak was suggested by Eastman as being short, punchy and easily pronounced throughout the world. He also thought that the name sounded like the clicking of a camera shutter. The camera itself was a box type, which took roll film with 100 exposures (too many) and you had to log each exposure taken, as there was no frame counter. Though it was certainly revolutionary, the Kodak No 1 was expensive (5 guineas), and out of the reach of a huge potential market – Eastman's main target. In 1895 Eastman introduced the Pocket Kodak camera which took 12 exposures on a $1\frac{1}{2} \times 2$in roll-film cartridge, and the camera went on sale for 1 guinea. At the turn of the century Eastman unveiled the BROWNIE camera for photographers of all ages. It was of a $2\frac{1}{4} \times 2\frac{1}{4}$in format, and cost a mere 5 shillings.

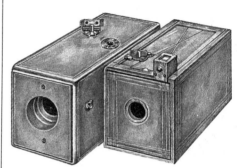

KODAK No 1.

Kostinsky effect

Development phenomenon whereby small areas in the image situated very close together shift relative to one another. It is caused by the same kind of exhaustion and displacement of developing solution that brings about EDGE EFFECTS. In the case of dense areas on a clear ground, the developer exhausts more rapidly between the areas than elsewhere, so that the edges of the areas are underdeveloped and in effect recede. In the case of light areas on a dense ground, the opposite effect takes place and the areas move nearer to each other.

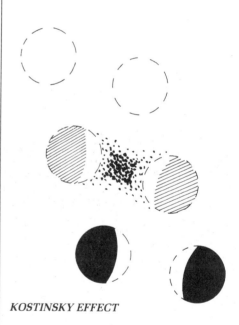

KOSTINSKY EFFECT

L

LASER

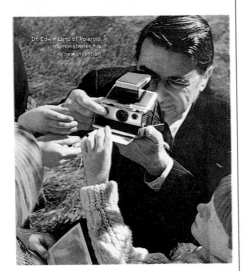

LAND, EDWIN

Lamphouse

Part of an enlarger or projector containing the lamp or light source. Since the lamp gives off considerable heat, the lamphouse is usually ventilated (and in the case of a projector cooled) by an electric fan. The lamphouse may also contain a heat filter, condenser, reflector and negative carrier. In colour enlargers, the lamphouse is additionally fitted with a set of filters, allowing precise control over the hues of the print.

Lanchester, F. W. see LIPPMAN

Land, Edwin

American founder of the Polaroid Corporation and inventor of the instant picture camera and system. In fact, the idea had been suggested to Land by his daughter, in 1940, who wanted – as most photographers want – to see the results of the exposure *at once*. But as every inventor discovers, nothing is really new. In the 1890s there was a camera called the 'NODARK', which processed its own film in the camera. The Nodark merely developed the negative, whereas Land's revolutionary invention produced a positive print in minutes. Land's film contained a pod of reagent which broke when the film was pulled out of the camera after exposure. The reagent dissolved and developed the unexposed halides, which migrated on to a receiving layer and formed a black and white positive print. Land then progressed by introducing a subtractive colour dye transfer process which used a similar technique of dye migration. It was based on the TRIPACK principle and in Land's invention the reagents liberated dyes adjacent to the unexposed halides. The colour dyes migrated to the receiving layer to form a positive coloured image. Instant photography was introduced by Land in 1947, in Boston, Massachusetts, while Instant Color film was introduced in 1963.

Lantern slide

Rather archaic term for a projection slide or transparency. It dates from the time when projectors were called magic lanterns.

Large-format camera see page 96

Laser

Acronym for Light Amplification by Stimulated Emission of Radiation, describing a device for producing an intense beam of coherent light of a single very pure colour. Lasers are used in the production of holograms and in various fields of scientific photography. A technique has also been recently developed for making colour prints from transparencies by using lasers to produce from a 35mm transparency a set of electronic signals that can be processed to produce a print. Blue, green and red lasers pass through the transparency and generate electronic signals according to the proportions and densities of the colours in the image; the signals are processed in a computer and used to drive three more lasers that make an exposure on high-resolution, fine-grain film that can be processed in the normal way. This laser process, which is available commercially, produces prints of a quality comparable with those obtained by the dye transfer process but is quicker and also cheaper per print. It is also possible to use the process to produce a variety of special effects by distorting the colour values of the image.

Latensification

Intensification of the latent image, a process similar to HYPERSENSITIZING but differing in that it is carried out after exposure and before development of the negative. Latensification may be carried out with a chemical solution or a chemical vapour and also by exposure to light. In effect it is a method of boosting the emulsion speed of negatives that have suffered from

RECIPROCITY LAW FAILURE through very long exposure to weak light or very short exposure to insufficient light. Exposing the latent image to additional light at low intensities increases image density only in areas where the image already exists, and although some overall fog is also formed, this is more than compensated for by the gain in image intensity that the process produces.

Latent image

Invisible image recorded on photographic emulsion as a result of exposure to light. The latent image is converted into a visible image by the action of a developer. The manner by which the physical formation of the latent image takes place is still not clearly established, but it may be that atoms of silver coagulate or concentrate through the influence of actinic light to form nuclei of silver specks. The increase in growth of these specks depends on the relative intensity of the light and it appears that a foundation of receptive nuclei is necessary to establish growth and image formation. Weak light fails to create a sufficiently stable foundation upon which to build a strong image, resulting in RECIPROCITY LAW FAILURE, often encountered when very short exposures are used.

Lateral chromatic aberration see
ABERRATION

Latitude see EXPOSURE LATITUDE

LCD (Liquid Crystal Display)

Electronic numerical indicator that displays shutter speeds and apertures in the viewfinder of certain SLR cameras, relating directly to the camera's exposure control. LCD systems, which are also used in other photographic apparatus such as hand-held exposure meters, have the advantage over LEDs of using less battery power but the disadvantages of

being less easily visible in dim lighting conditions and suffering in temperature extremes. At high temperatures (above about 60°C) the display turns black, clearing as it cools down, and at low temperatures (below about −10°C) the liquid crystals become more viscose, causing the reaction time of the display to slow down.

Leaf shutter

An alternative term for between-the-lens SHUTTER.

LED (Light Emitting Diode)

Solid state electrical component used as a glowing coloured indicator inside a camera VIEWFINDER or other photographic apparatus to provide a visual signal or warning indicator for various controls. The most common use of LEDs is to provide exposure information in viewfinders. This is done most simply by a light glowing when exposure is correct, and in its most sophisticated form by a display of digital figures indicating aperture, shutter speed and other factors such as whether flash is being used.

Leica

Classic German camera and one of the first to use 35mm format film, for which the camera was designed. The Leica was invented by OSCAR BARNACK, who saw the need for a 'small negative, big picture' camera. His first design, in 1905, was a 5 × 7in plate camera modified to take 20 exposures on one roll of film. Barnack experimented with motion picture film and in 1912 drew up the designs for a slim, 35mm camera. Two prototypes, the original UR-Leicas as they became known, were made in 1913, one used by Barnack, the other by Barnack's employer, Ernst Leitz. In fact, Barnack had originally offered the design to Carl Zeiss, who failed to see the camera's potential, so it went to Leitz, in Wetzlar, where the only surviving

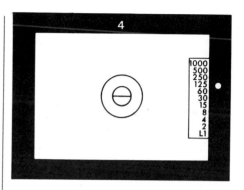

LED: Light emitting diodes are designed to convey information with symbols and numbers on the viewing screen of SLR cameras.

LEICA: The Leica, with its use of 35mm film, pointed the way to a new style of photography – that of photo-reportage, the "grabbed" shot by available light. The quiet shutter and fast lenses appealed to such photographers as Cartier-Bresson and the Vogue and Newsweek photographer the late Jack Nisberg, described as a "Leica man up to the hilt."

Large format cameras

General term applied to cameras using large sheet film negatives, now usually 5×4in and above, although smaller formats such as $3\frac{1}{4} \times 4\frac{1}{4}$ (quarter-plate) are also still used. Large-format cameras come in many shapes and sizes, but they all share certain characteristics. They focus by means of extensible bellows running between front and rear panels. The front panel holds the lens, the rear panel a ground glass screen, which is displaced by a DARK SLIDE containing film when the exposure is to be made. Interchangeable lenses usually have integral diaphragms and shutter mechanisms. Images on the focusing screen are inverted and reversed left to right, but some cameras take a focusing hood with an angled mirror that corrects the image to appear the right way up. The various names applied to different types of large-format camera tend to be used with a confusing degree of interchangeability and lack of precision. The clearest distinction that can be made is between monorail and baseboard cameras. Monorail cameras have a sturdy tube or rail on which the bellows and panels slide, with a locking mechanism to clamp them firm. They provide the greatest possible control over the image, having a complete range of camera movements and the capacity for variable extension by the addition of extra bellows and rail elements – there is no camera 'body' as such. In baseboard cameras, the lens panel and bellows move on twin rails on a baseboard that folds up against the rear panel when the camera is not in use, making the unit comparatively compact and portable. Baseboard cameras have more restricted movements than monorail cameras, sometimes limited to rising and falling front. The terms field camera and view camera are used for large-format cameras designed to be portable enough for regular work in the field, and they are thus more or less synonymous with baseboard camera. The term studio camera now tends to

be restricted to the very large and solid type of apparatus hardly met with outside the establishments of professional portrait photographers. Technical camera is a term used virtually synonymously with large-format camera, and the term plate camera is still often encountered used in the same fashion, although all modern large-format cameras, of course, take sheet film rather than glass plates.

Large format cameras, although weighty and far from compact when compared to the medium formats, are extremely flexible. The camera movements, allow considerable control over the image, especially valuable in studio work and architectural photography, **left**.

lens from light coming from areas outside the field of view. Such light is one of the sources of FLARE. Lens hoods are designed specifically for each focal length of lens, giving an angle of view slightly larger than the lens's. A hood made for a long focal length lens would cut off the field of view of a wide-angle or standard lens, and as a general rule the shorter the focal length, the shallower the depth of the hood. Rectangular hoods are more efficient than round ones.

Lens mount

Mechanism on an interchangeable lens for fitting it to the camera body. There are two main kinds of lens mount – screw thread and bayonet: the former, as the name suggests, screws into the camera body; the latter locks the lens into position by slotting a flange (bayonet) into a groove and giving the lens a short twist. Bayonet lenses have now virtually eclipsed screw lenses as they are quicker to use and can more easily accommodate the sophisticated linkages necessary to convey information between body and lens in modern battery-powered automatic cameras. Many independent manufacturers make lenses with a choice of mounts, and adapters are also available to enable various lenses to be fitted to cameras other than those for which their mounts are matched.

Lenticular system

System of small lenses of equal size and shape combined for the purpose of gathering and concentrating light or for breaking up an image that can later be recombined by a matching lenticular screen. The system is similar to that found in the compound eye of a fly. Lenticular lenses and screens have various uses in photography. In some exposure meters – the Weston Master, for example – a lenticular lens covers the photoelectric cell to gather lightwaves and determine the angle of acceptance. Lenticular screens are

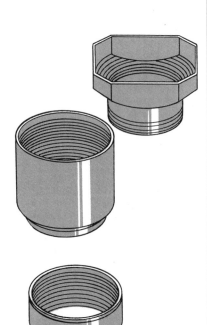

LENS HOODS

UR-Leica is preserved. Thirty prototypes were constructed before the Model A made its debut at the Leipzig Spring Fair, in 1925. The company had decided to call it 'The Leca' after LEitz CAmera, but by 1925 it had changed to Leica. The first model was fitted with an f3.5, 50mm Anastigmat lens. Subsequent cameras had first Elmax, then Elmar lenses. The focal plane shutter gave speeds from 1/20th second to 1/500th second, and a novel feature was the wind-on knob which simultaneously tensioned the shutter – a truly fast, 'action' camera which revolutionized PHOTOJOURNALISM, especially when Leica added an integral rangefinder, in the Leica 11 model. Even today these early Leicas are remarkably slim, compact and finely engineered, while today's version has, in the opinion of one writer, 'charisma' without sacrificing the traditional Leica quality.

Lens see page 100

Lens hood/shade

Simple lens accessory, usually made of thin metal or rubber, used to shield the employed to produce stereoscopic images and for projection purposes.

Light

Visible ELECTROMAGNETIC radiation, the natural agent that arouses the sense of sight. The visible part of the electromagnetic spectrum, from red to violet, encompasses wavelengths between 4,000 and 7,000Å (400–700nm), the colour of the light being determined by the length of the wave. Blue light, for example, has a shorter wavelength than red. The waves at the blue-violet end of the spectrum are the more highly ACTINIC, that is they more strongly affect the photographic emulsion. Infrared and ultraviolet waves, invisible to the human eye, can be recorded on specially sensitized films.

Light box

Large flat box with an opaque glass top, illuminated from below, and useful for viewing a selection of slides, or strips of negatives.

Light units

Values used to measure light according to its intensity, colour or quality. Wavelengths are measured in Ångstroms (Å) or nanometres (nm), the former being one ten-millionth of a millimetre, the latter a millionth of a millimetre (ten Ångstroms). These units enable colours to be identified and defined scientifically. Blue-green light, for example, has a wavelength of 5,000Å (500nm). Light can also be measured according to its COLOUR TEMPERATURE in Kelvins (K) or on the MIRED scale. The intensity of light can be measured at its source; as it falls upon a subject (incident light); or as it is reflected from a subject. Light emission was originally measured by candle power related to the intensity of a specified wax candle burned under controlled conditions. This was replaced by the CANDELA, defined in terms of the radiating power of a

BLACK BODY at a specified temperature. Incident light is measured in lumens, one lumen being the luminous flux or light flow measured on one square metre of a subject's surface placed a metre away from a point source of one candela. The light of one candela reflected from one square metre is known as a foot lambert or nit. Many other terms are used in the scientific study of light, but they are rarely encountered in practical photography.

Line film

Type of film similar to LITH FILM but producing even sharper edges when greatly enlarged. Line film is slightly more expensive than lith film, but it has the advantage of possessing greater exposure latitude. It is used principally in the graphics industry for copying work where maximum clarity of definition is necessary.

Liquid Crystal Display see LCD

Lippman process

A technique of colour photography first demonstrated in 1891 by Gabriel Lippman, French professor of physics at the Sorbonne in Paris, and inventor of the INTERFERENCE process of photography. The process was an early attempt at presenting a colour image by exploiting the phenomena of 'standing' lightwaves. Interference photography bears some resemblance to the Daguerreotype, and the hologram, in that the image in each case needs to be viewed from a certain angle and in a favourable light. At the time Lippman's invention generated considerable interest, although it was fundamentally impractical because the process demanded exceptionally long exposures. The phenomenon of standing waves was first examined by Wilhelm Zenker in 1868. It occurs naturally in thin films of oil, and in mother of pearl that show an iridescent spectra caused when arriving lightwaves collide with those

Moral

Little girls, this seems to say,
Never stop upon your way.
Never trust a stranger-friend;
No one knows how it will end.
As you're pretty, so be wise;
Wolves may lurk in every guise.
Handsome they may be, and kind,
Gay, or charming—never mind!
Now, as then, 'tis simple truth—
Sweetest tongue has sharpest tooth!

LINE FILM

Lens

Device of glass or other transparent material used to form images by bending and focusing rays of light. Light travels more slowly through the solid material of the lens than through air, so that rays of light, other than those travelling along the lens's AXIS, are bent, or refracted, both on entering the lens and on leaving it. As well as bending light, a lens also DISPERSES it, the blue component, for example, emerging at a different angle to the red.

In spite of the new wave of lightweight "standard" zoom lenses, the standard remains the prime lens fitted to most SLRs, and are useful for their wide maximum apertures.

*Lenses below are, **left:** zoom lens which can range in focal length from wide angle to long focus; **centre:** telephoto lens, and **right:** catadioptric or mirror lens.*

Macro lenses are used for extreme close-up photography at a ratio of 1:1.

Fisheye lenses can have angles of view as wide as 180°, but giving distorted circular images.

Shift and tilt lenses control perspective and can eliminate unwanted peripheral areas of the image.

The refractive and dispersive power of a lens depends on the composition of the glass and on the lens's shape, and lenses are grouped into two main types according to shape – converging and diverging. A converging, or positive, lens bends light rays to meet at a point on the axis of the lens; a diverging, or negative, lens bends light rays to spread away from the axis. Converging lenses are thicker at the centre than at the edges, and thus essentially convex; diverging lenses are thicker at the edges than the centre, and so essentially concave. One of the surfaces may also be flat, and according to the arrangement of convex, concave or flat surfaces, lenses may be classified into six different kinds – biconvex, planoconvex, concavo-convex, biconcave, plano-concave and convexo-concave. Most lenses are biconvex, and the word 'lens' in fact derives from the Latin for lentil (*lens*) because of the similarity in shape. The OPTICAL GLASS used in lenses is of two main types: flint glass possesses a high refractive index and high degree of dispersion; crown glass combines a high refractive index with low dispersion. A single lens cannot produce an image that is acceptably accurate for normal photographic purposes, and the principal aim of the lens designer is to combine separate pieces of glass (elements) into a compound lens that reduces ABERRATIONS to a minimum. A standard lens for a 35mm camera

usually has about six elements; a ZOOM lens may have well over a dozen elements. The calculations necessary to determine suitable curvatures for the glass surfaces involve the tracing of the paths of thousands of imaginary rays of light through various elements. Today this is done by computer, but originally involved extraordinarily painstaking computations by hand. The Hungarian mathematician JOSEF PETZVAL, who in 1840 designed the celebrated lens named after him (the first lens to be designed in the modern sense rather than created by a process of mechanical trial and error), is said to have obtained the services of a company of military engineers to assist

him with his calculations. Grinding and polishing of lenses must also be carried out with extreme accuracy to ensure optimum optical performance. Assessing the quality of a lens involves the consideration of many different factors, which goes some way to explain why evaluations of the same lens in different photographic journals may vary considerably. The factors taken into consideration usually include resolving power, degree of contrast and balance of aberrations. A lens giving good contrast may produce an image that to the subjective human eye looks sharper than one produced by a lens with higher resolving power but giving weaker contrast.

The reflex or mirror lens is based on the catadioptric principle which uses a combination of lenses and mirrors.

LIPPMAN, GABRIEL: French scientist and inventor of a remarkable direct colour process, which however, proved impractical.

LUMIERE BROTHERS

reflected by an underlying reflective backing. The stationary waves form peaks and troughs in layers, or laminae, in the surface film that coats the backing. While light is not reflected by the troughs, the peaks create a visible and strong rendering of the colour transmitted by the particular wavelength. One of the first experimenters to demonstrate the theory was Otto Weiner in 1889, who used a photographic emulsion in contact with a reflective surface. The Lippman process improved on previous experiments, and is one of the very few direct colour photographic techniques. Today's colour pictures are produced by an indirect method – the 'tripack' emulsion layers of dyes only approximate the natural colours of the scene. Direct colour recording is achieved by capturing the frequency of lightwaves (every lightwave transmits colour according to the frequency of the wave – blue, for example, has a very short frequency, while red lightwaves are long), as in the Lippman process, or by prismatic dispersion of the spectrum, as in Lanchester's process of 1895. Here, the image through the lens was passed through a very fine screen, and via a series of elements and prisms, to reach a photographic plate. The screen split the arriving lightwaves into minute spectra according to the colour and intensity of the wave. A positive transparency in black and white was made, then viewed by a reverse system and backlit. Thus it bore some resemblance to the additive colour screens where screen and positive transparency are viewed together. In the Lippman process, the colour image was formed in the emulsion itself. Where standing waves peak in an emulsion that colour is recorded by exposure of the silver halides, because the peaks create light, the troughs do not – so a 'blue' peak would establish a blue-sensitive record in the silver. When viewed, incident light falling on the plate would produce a blue response, when short wavelengths of the blue frequency 'recognized' the blue record, provided that the plate had a reflective backing and the viewing angle was favourable. Colour records were established at different levels in the emulsion, according to the frequency. Thus in the Lippman plate, where standing waves were created by a mercury backing, a coloured strata was produced.

Lith film

Ultra-high-contrast film used to eliminate grey half-tones and produce an image of pure black and white areas. The film has a very thin coat of emulsion, producing extreme contrast, sharpness and speed, and is designed to be processed with a special lith developer based on formaldehyde-hydroquinone. Lith films are used in graphic design to convert half-tone drawings, or photographs, into line, and in the reproduction of printed matter to produce both line and screen negatives and positives from which the printing plates can be made.

Local control see BURNING IN and DODGING

In printing, giving specific parts of the print more or less exposure than the rest.

Long-focus lens

Lens with a FOCAL LENGTH greater than that of the standard lens for a given format. As a standard lens has a focal length approximately equal to the diagonal of the film format it covers, a long-focus lens may also be defined as one with a focal length greater than this diagonal. Long-focus lenses have a narrow field of view and make distant objects appear closer; the longer the focal length, the greater the magnification and narrower the angle of view. In order to decrease their length, many long-focus lenses have a TELEPHOTO construction.

Long Tom

Colloquial term for a large, high-powered long-focus lens.

Lumière, Auguste and Louis

French inventors and champions of colour photography, and of the LIPPMAN PROCESS. They were pioneers of the cinema, and with their fine-quality AUTOCHROME colour plates did much to encourage a colour awareness, especially in the amateur market. They were one of the first to successfully launch a subtractive colour-printing process, using BICHROMATED GELATIN exposed under separation negatives and toned with complementary colours. But their greatest work lies in the realm of cinematography, where they showed the way by using 35mm celluloid film, in a camera of their own design with a rachet and claw to advance the film.

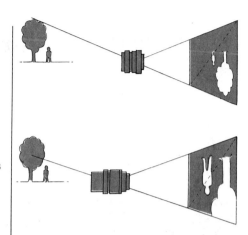

*LONG FOCUS LENS: Magnification is proportional to focal length, so an image from a 100m lens will be twice proportionate to that from a 50mm standard lens (**top**).*

LITH FILM

McDonough, James
American inventor of a colour screen plate patented in 1896, and similar to the JOLY process. McDonough used very finely ruled red, blue and green lines on glass plates, but manufacturing techniques were unable to produce the high standards of accuracy needed. According to McDonough, the perfect screen plate was one in which the colours were so perfectly balanced that upon viewing appeared as if entirely free of colour, which McDonough termed the 'first black condition'. Although some of McDonough's screen plates were of excellent quality, he was unable to realize them commercially. In an effort to produce a less exacting screen, McDonough devised a plate dusted with dyed, powdered shellac to be coated with a sensitive emulsion, a technique that foreshadowed Lumière's Autochrome plate that used grains of randomly-scattered potato starch.

Mackie line
Line appearing around a highlight on a silver halide emulsion. It is produced by the lateral diffusion of exhausted developer that causes EDGE EFFECTS. The increased density at the edge of a high-density area and the reduced density at the edge of a low-density area give the effect of a lighter line around the dense image area. The Mackie line is not usually obvious except in extreme circumstances, and is particularly associated with the SABATTIER EFFECT.

Macro lens
Term used to describe any close-focusing lens, although strictly speaking it should be confined to ones

MACRO PHOTOGRAPHY

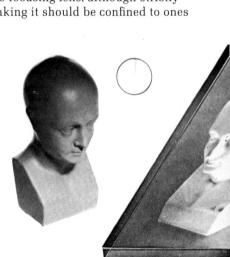

capable of giving 1:1 (life-size) or larger magnifications. Macro lenses can also be used for normal photography at ordinary subject distances.

Macrophotography

The production of giant photographs, for example as posters or mural decoration. Although this is the strict definition of the term, it is more commonly used to refer to close-up photography, for which the correct term is photomacrography. The usage is so widespread, however, that it would be pedantic to attempt to discontinue it.

Maddox, Richard Leach

English physician, amateur photographer and inventor of the gelatin dry plate. Maddox's emulsion was too crude for commercial application, and JOHN BURGESS, to whom the first practical dry plate must be accorded, stated that Maddox had 'laid no claim to having made a great discovery, he simply recorded an abortive experiment'. The experiment, described in 1871, was the first use of GELATIN as a substitute for COLLODION, where the gelatin could be effectively sensitized. This was achieved by the interaction of cadmium bromide with silver nitrate that produced silver bromide in the gelatin. This emulsion was used on glass plates for negatives, certainly the first gelatin-bromide negatives ever made, but they were of less than pefect definition, and contain a percentage of crystalline salts that marred the quality.

Magazine

Interchangeable, preloading film carrier that locks on to the back of a roll-film or 35mm cassette camera, allowing for quick change of film type or format or quick renewal of film during shooting – often invaluable aids for professional work. Bulk film magazines can hold up to 250 exposures thus making frequent pauses for reloading unnecessary.

Magenta

One of the three colours in the SUBTRACTIVE SYNTHESIS, also known as minus-green. Magenta, the complementary colour to green, is formed by the combination of red and blue lightwaves, the addition of green making white light. Subtracting green from white light gives magenta, hence the term 'minus-green'.

Magnification

Ratio of image size to object size, or the lens-to-image distance to the subject-to-lens distance. The magnification ratio is sometimes useful in determining the correct exposure in close-up and macrophotography.

MAGENTA

MADDOX

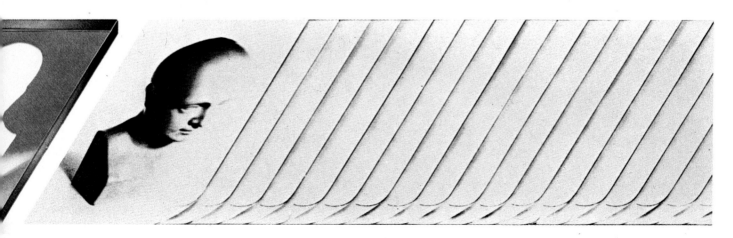

Mandala

Image made of many identical elements arranged in a regular, repeating pattern. Mandalas can be produced photographically, using photo-montage techniques, multiple printing, or by making a multiple exposure in a copy camera from duplicates of the original.

Manly, Thomas see CARBON PROCESS

English photographer whose work with BICHROMATED GELATIN led to his inventing the 'Ozobrome' or Carbro process.

Mannes and Godowsky

American inventors of the first commercial integral tripack film. Launched in April 1935 in the form of a 16mm reversal movie film it was called Kodachrome. Leopold Mannes and Leopold Godowsky were Harvard graduates and professional musicians – Godowsky played the violin and Mannes the piano. Their partnership as musicians was also complemented by their partnership as photographers, and their mutual interest in colour photography – while all photographers were aware of the potential of colour, in the 1920s a practical and versatile film seemed a long way off. Through the auspices of C. Kenneth Mees of Eastman Kodak, Mannes and Godowsky joined the Kodak Research Laboratory, where they experimented with two-layer and three-layer emulsions. The idea of a tripack had been around for some twenty years, but a practical solution had yet to be found. Much work had been done by Agfa's RUDOLF FISCHER, but progress was hampered by the fact that the dyes, or colour couplers, tended to wander haphazardly through the tripack layers. Mannes and Godowsky employed a bit of lateral scientific thinking. Why not, they reasoned, put the colour couplers in the *developer*? This was, and still remains, the technique used in the processing of Kodachrome film, and is the basis of the C-14 process, which requires a controlled diffusion bleach of the silver image, and the complex addition of dye formers.

Marey, Etienne Jules

French physiologist and great exponent (with Eadweard Muybridge) of action photography and camera techniques. Marey's prime interest was in the analysis of movement in humans and animals, and in 1882 he devised a photographic gun for taking pictures of birds in flight. The gun remains one of the most remarkable – and advanced – cameras in photographic history. It had an adjustable telephoto lens in the barrel, a rifle stock, and a magazine like a revolver for holding the plates. These were discs (25 to each magazine) with 12 gelatin emulsion exposures around the rim (predating Kodak's DISC CAMERA by over a century!). The plate revolved on

MAREY CHRONOPHOTOGRAPHIC CAMERA, 1882

pressing the trigger to give 12 exposures per second at 1/720 second per exposure. Marey followed his gun in 1887 with a chronophotographic camera that took 60 shots per second on celluloid roll film at 1/1000th second. This camera not only led to the progressive development of the cine camera, but foreshadows the motor drive systems of today. A detailed account of Marey's experiments can be found in his book *Le Mouvement*, 1884, and translated into English.

Masking
Term used to describe various ways in which light is prevented from reaching selected areas of an image for various purposes. Some enlargers, for example, have masking devices built into their carrier – metal strips that can be adjusted so that only the exact part of the negative or transparency that you wish to print will be projected. More complex types of masking occur in SANDWICHING.

Masking frame
Frame placed beneath the enlarger lens (usually on the enlarger baseboard) to establish print size, determine proportions of the picture and keep the printing paper flat. It may also be adjustable to provide white borders around the print.

Matrix
Gelatin relief image used to transfer colour to paper in certain printing processes such as the dye transfer process. The gelatin has a raised or embossed surface, similar to that used in letterpress printing.

Matte
Opaque strip or plate used in MASKING during exposure or printing.

Maxwell, James Clerk
Prominent Scottish scientist and inventor who produced the world's first colour photograph in order to

demonstrate the physical principles of THOMAS YOUNG's colour theory. The photograph was first shown in the Royal Institution, London, in 1861. To achieve his now famous picture of a tartan ribbon, Clerk Maxwell and his assistant Thomas Sutton exposed three collodion plates, each through a different primary filter of red, green, and blue-violet. The processed images were then projected by three projectors containing matching primary filters, and so aligned that the images were placed in register, thus a full colour photograph was obtained by the ADDITIVE SYNTHESIS. Clerk Maxwell's experiment raised the question: how did he manage to record the red/violet stripes of the tartan, since the plate would have been insensitive to red? This was, remember, in the pre-panchromatic era before the red-sensitizing dye PINACYANOL had been found. Then a Kodak researcher, Ralph Evans, discovered in 1961 that the red parts of the ribbon coincidentally transmitted UV waves, and were recorded as 'red' on the plate.

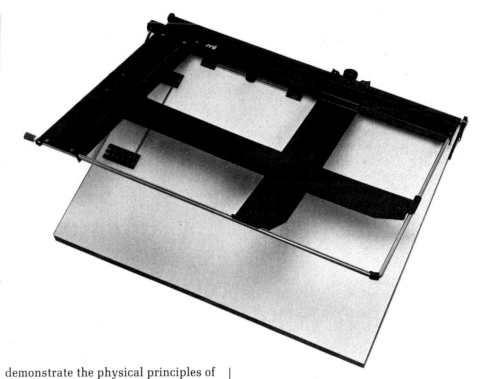

MASKING FRAME: To hold the paper perfectly flat, and give accurate measurements, frames should be sturdy and with calibrations along the abutments.

CLERK MAXWELL: Maxwell was one of the great scientists of the 19th century whose contribution to photography was for him of minor importance, beside his more weighty theories of electro-magnetism, gases and heat.

Medium-format camera

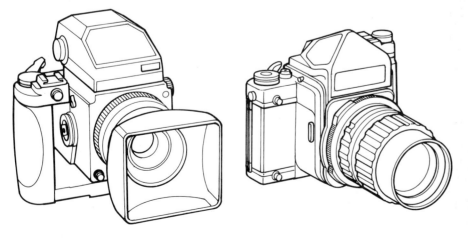

Term applied to cameras taking roll-film and producing a negative or transparency between approximately 6 × 4.5cm and 6 × 9cm. Medium-format cameras therefore come in size between MINIATURE and LARGE-FORMAT CAMERAS. There are three main kinds of medium-format camera: (1) the single-lens reflex, of which there are types used at both waist and eye level; (2) the twin-lens reflex; (3) non-reflex models, the most popular type of which is rather like an enlarged 35mm rangefinder camera except that its lens panel is fitted to extensible bellows.

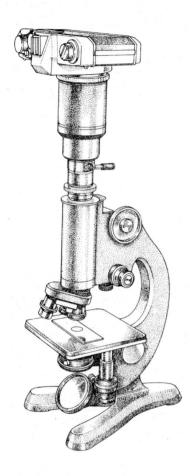

MICROPHOTOGRAPHY: Like many techniques in photography, microphotography is by no means a newcomer – J.B. Dancer made pictures through a microscope in the 1850's. Today, however, the technique has considerable scientific value, especially in the storage of information; a large area of fine print, such as a newspaper, can be stored on film, and on microfiche sheets.

Mercury vapour lamp

Light source sometimes used in studio photography, giving a greenish light produced by passing an electric current through a tube filled with mercury vapour.

Metol

Developing agent, available under various brand names. It is a white crystalline powder, and can cause allergic reaction.

Microflash

Flash of light of extremely short duration. Microflashes are obtained by using light sources such as a pulsed laser beam, and are operated in conjunction with special shutters such as a Kerr cell (see SHUTTER).

Micrograph

A photograph taken through a microscope. It is a shortened form of the more correct term, photomicrograph.

Microphotography

Technique used to copy documents and similar materials on to very small format film so that a large amount of information may be stored compactly. Special cameras are used for microfilming. The most common type is somewhat similar in appearance to an enlarger, the camera unit being attached to an upright column on which it can be moved up and down to give various reductions, while the document is placed flat on a baseboard in the same position as an enlarging easel. Lights are built-in on arms on each side of the central column. Exposure is usually automatic, with a variable-speed shutter, and a typical lens has a focal length of 28mm and an aperture of f4.5. Film, which must have a very fine grain and high resolving power, comes in long rolls of various widths, usually of 16mm or 35mm format. The processed film is stored either in rolls or on small sheets of film called microfiche, both types being read on special viewers that project the image on to a screen, enlarging it to approximately original size. Large table viewers are now common features in libraries, and portable viewers, folding to the size of a small attaché case, are also available. It is also possible to project microfiche images on to a large-scale screen, so they can be used to illustrate lectures or demonstrations. Fiche come in various sizes; a typical one is the size of a postcard (approximately 4 × 6in) and contains 60 frames. An advantage of fiche over microfilm in rolls is that the material is easier to handle, it being possible to scan the film with the naked eye to locate particular images. While rolls of microfilm are highly suitable for recording rare books or other printed material, fiche are better for subjects where there is more variation in the individual images, such as, for example, photographs of works of art. The art collections of major museums such as the Victoria and Albert Museum and the Wallace Collection in London have been recorded on microfiche in this way, the microfiche format being so compact that more than 10,000 eye-legible images can be stored in an easily accessible form in a simple 12 × 10in binder. Microfiche (frequently computer generated) are also extensively used in trade and industry, recording, for example, customer lists and banking transactions.

Microprism

A small prism. A series of microprisms is used moulded into the standard focusing screens of most 35mm SLRs to assist focusing, the image appearing to shimmer when out of focus. The microprisms are usually arranged in a central ring or 'collar'. Some photographers consider them more a hindrance than a help, and prefer the viewing screens of their cameras to be as uncluttered as possible.

Miniature camera

Term applied to cameras with a film format of 35mm or less. It dates from the time when almost all serious photography was carried out on larger-format cameras, and since 35mm is now the most common format for both professional and amateur use, the term is falling into disuse.

Mired

Acronym for Micro-Reciprocal Degree, a unit of COLOUR TEMPERATURE used to calibrate colour correction filters. The mired value of a light source is found by dividing one million by the source's colour temperature in Kelvins. A filter's ability to change the colour quality of a light source, expressed as a plus or minus number of micro-reciprocal degrees, is called its mired shift value. Filters are assigned fixed mired shift values by which they will modify the mired value of the light source. Yellowish filters have positive mired shift values, which means that they raise the mired value of the light source and lower its colour temperature. Bluish filters have negative values, lowering the mired value of the light source and raising the colour temperature. A decamired is ten mireds – a colour shift of a magnitude that can just be detected by the human eye.

Mirror lens

Lens of long focal length that uses mirrors within its construction to make it more physically compact than a lens of the same focal length of normal construction. The path of light is 'folded' by the mirrors, making the lens much shorter than its counterpart, and because mirrors replace some of the glass elements, it is also much lighter. Mirror lenses also reduce aberrations, because when light is reflected from a mirror it is not refracted as it is when passing through a lens. Against these obvious advantages must be set the drawback that mirror lenses have a

fixed aperture – typically f8 for a 500mm lens. Under very bright conditions this problem can be overcome to some extent by using neutral density filters to reduce the amount of light entering the lens, but this will not change the depth of field, as would altering the physical aperture. The construction of mirror lenses produces a distinctive – and often very attractive – effect with out-of-focus highlights, the patches of light being ring shaped rather than continuous discs as are the ones created by lenses of normal construction. The effect is caused by the blank spot resulting from the positioning of the front mirror in the centre of the front element of the lens. The term catadioptric lens is often used interchangeably with mirror lens, but strictly speaking a catadioptric lens is only one type of mirror lens. A catadioptric lens uses mirrors and lenses; the other type, called a catoptric lens, uses only mirrors.

Mirror lock

Facility found on some advanced 35mm SLR cameras for holding the reflex mirror in the 'up' position. The

MINIATURE CAMERAS

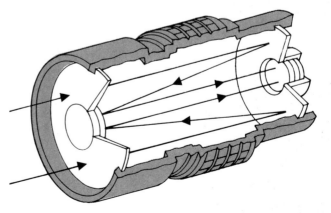

MIRROR LENS

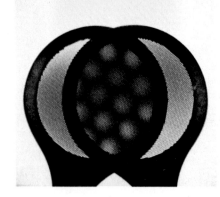

MOIRE

mirror lock is used in three different situations. First, some extreme WIDE-ANGLE lenses extend so far into the camera body as to obstruct the movement of the mirror in its normal position, so it must be locked up when the lens is used. Secondly, the mirror lock can be used during extreme precision work to minimize vibration during the exposure. Finally, the mirror lock can be used when a MOTOR-DRIVE is fitted to the camera, so that the time taken by the mirror to rise and return to its original position does not prevent the motor-drive from operating at its highest rate of frames per second. When the mirror is locked up it is obviously impossible to view the image through the normal viewfinder, but in this situation an accessory viewfinder can be fitted to the camera's hot shoe.

Moiré
The effect produced when identical patterns are superimposed slightly out of register, producing a shimmering quality resembling moiré silk. Interesting moiré effects can be produced in SANDWICHING.

Monobath
Combination of developer and fixer in a single solution for the rapid one-stage processing of black and white film. The process takes only three to four minutes, and so is useful when speed is of the essence or for convenience on location. With the latest type, a 35mm film can be processed in the cassette and in daylight, the film being simply dropped into a container of the solution; a disadvantage is loss of contrast due to slight fogging.

Monochromatic
Light of a single or limited band of wavelengths, but a term used principally to identify an image or picture having a range of tones of a single hue or tones on black and white.

Monopod
A one-legged camera support, usually telescopic. Although obviously less stable than a TRIPOD, a monopod is a useful piece of equipment in certain circumstances, particularly where space is cramped. When photographing from a crowd, for example, the monopod can be braced against the photographer's body or can be used to lift the camera above obstructions, the shutter being operated with a long CABLE RELEASE. Monopods are used by sports photographers in conjunction with long-focus lenses and fast film to eliminate CAMERA SHAKE.

Montage
Composite picture made from several different photographic images cut out and mounted on a single piece of paper or other support. Montage is used in making panoramas and mosaic pictures (as in aerial surveys, for example), and is one of the most common techniques used in trick photography. The image produced is frequently rephotographed so that the joins between separate parts of the picture are inconspicuous. The term montage is sometimes extended to cover COMBINATION PRINTING.

Mosaic
Type of montage consisting of an assembly of separate photographs making a continuous image. Used in aerial reconnaissance, cartography and to make panoramic views.

Motor-drive see also INTERVALOMETER and page 114

MQ/PQ developers
Popular developing agents based on a combination of metol and hydroquinone, or Phenidone and hydroquinone. The developers are all-purpose, producing good, strong blacks and warm tones on film negatives and on bromide papers.

MTF (Modulation Transfer Function)
Method of evaluating the sharpness of
lenses by plotting on a graph the ratio
of subject/image contrast against the
image resolution. To the experienced
eye, the graph contains more
information about lens quality than a
conventional set of resolution figures.

Multigrade paper

Ilford trade name for a type of
variable-contrast paper, used to print
negatives of varying degrees of
contrast by means of changing filters
in the enlarger. This variation is made
possible by Multigrade's special
emulsion, which has a mixture of two
types of SILVER HALIDE, one sensitive to
blue light, the other to green light.
Exposing the blue-sensitive part
produces a high-contrast image;
exposing the green-sensitive part
produces a low-contrast image. Yellow
filters are used to absorb blue light and
transmit green, magenta filters to
absorb green and transmit blue. An
enlarger with a colour-mixing head can
be used to print on Multigrade paper,
but greater control is possible with
special Multigrade filters, which come
in a set of varying densities of yellow
and magenta. It is, of course, also
possible to print on Multigrade using
no filter at all. Multigrade paper is of
particular advantage to photographers
who do not do a great deal of printing,
because if several grades of paper were
kept, the little-used ones would tend to
go stale. It is also useful for printing
difficult negatives, as by skilful local
control and changing of filters it is
possible to have part of the image
effectively on soft paper and part of it
effectively on contrasty paper. Other
manufacturers sell a similar product
under a different name. Kodak's paper,
for example, is called 'Polycontrast'.

Multi-mode camera

SLR camera offering three or more
'modes' (systems of exposure control) –
manual, aperture priority, shutter
priority and 'programmed' being the
most common (see AUTOMATIC
EXPOSURE). Multi-mode cameras
require extremely sophisticated
electronics, and are a recent
innovation, the first – the Minolta XD7
– being introduced in 1977. The Canon
T90, introduced in 1986, offers the
most modes of any camera to date –
manual, stopped-down manual, shutter
priority, aperture priority,
stopped-down AE, flash AE, and seven
variable shift programs. Multi-mode
cameras are relatively expensive, but
because of their versatility already are
very popular.

Multiple exposure see also
CHROMOGRAPHOSCOPE, and under IVES,
FREDERICK
Technique of establishing two or more
images on one frame of film. Most
cameras, but not all, make provision
for multiple exposures so that a series
of images may be recorded without
winding on the film. Multiple exposure
can also refer to several identical
images on separate frames of film, and
juxtaposed to make a composite image,
as in the early colour cameras and
viewers.

MONTAGE

MONOPOD

Motor-drive

Battery-operated device for automatically advancing film in the camera and retensioning the shutter after an exposure has been made. The terms autowinder and motor-drive tend not to be used with great precision. Strictly, an autowinder is capable only of winding on the film a single frame at a time and not of rapid sequences, but in practice the term is generally used for units that can wind continuously at a rate of up to two frames per second (fps); for winders capable of higher speeds than this, the term motor-drive is used.

Power-winder is a somewhat vaguely used term, but generally it is construed as a synonym for autowinder. Almost all 35mm SLRs now accept an autowinder and/or motor-drive unit, and some medium-format SLRs accept autowinders. Cameras with built-in autowinders are made in both these formats. Almost all autowinders and motor-drives attach to the bottom of the camera, but they are rarely interchangeable between cameras, even on models made by the same manufacturer. Motordrives, which come into their own in fast-action sports photography, are much more expensive than autowinders, and the cameras to which they can be fitted must be more robustly built (more 'professional') than ones that accept only an autowinder because of the strain that the repeated vibration of its internal parts imposes on the camera. Several makers now produce cameras with built-in motordrive: Minolta, Olympus, Contax, Nikon, Canon, Pentax, etc. Most motor-drives have a maximum speed of 5fps, but Nikon make one capable of 6fps with the camera's mirror locked up. Faster speeds are available with special high-speed cameras such as the Nikon F2H, which is capable of 9fps, and Canon's amazing 14fps on the F-1, and 4.5fps on the T90. As a motor-driven camera operating at 5fps will run through a 36-exposure film in less than ten seconds, motor-drives are often used in conjunction with bulk film backs holding enough film for 250 exposures.

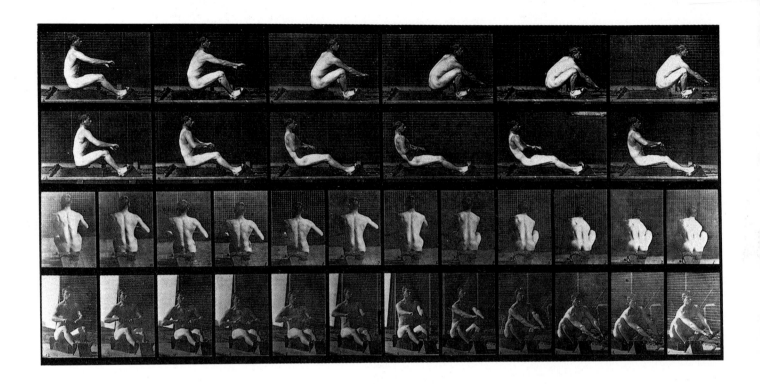

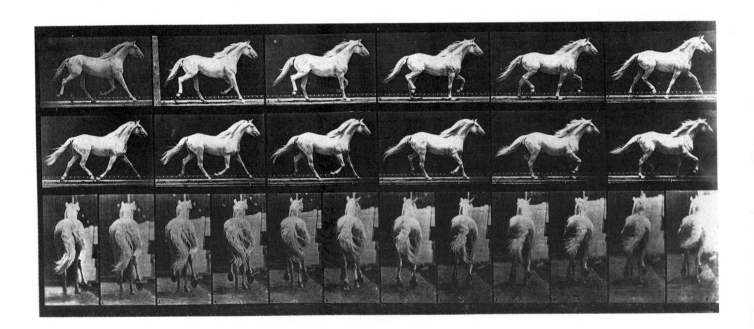

MUYBRIDGE

Munsell system

System of classifying and specifying colours published by the American scientist Albert Munsell in 1915 in his book *Atlas of the Munsell Color System*. Three factors are involved in Munsell's classification system: hue (the dominant wavelength of a colour – that is, the quality distinguishing, say, blueness from redness); value (lightness or darkness); and chroma (strength or purity – that is, the freedom from desaturation through admixture with white or from degradation through mixture with black). Theoretically, any colour can be specified by giving references for each of these factors. In practice, the system is employed mainly by paint chemists, who use the published colour samples as reference points.

Muybridge, Eadweard

Born Edward James Muggeridge, Muybridge was an English photographer working in America, and became Director of Photographic Surveys for the United States Government, largely as a result of his impressive pictures of landscapes, taken in the Yosemite Valley in 1867. He styled himself 'Helios, the flying camera' and was one of a select band of travel photographers of the 19th century who ventured into unknown territory (and not infrequently to the peaks of high mountains) to obtain pictures with large-format cameras – Muybridge's camera measured 22 × 28in. Muybridge is best remembered, though, for his work on action pictures (see also MAREY). Legend has it that this interest was triggered by an argument as to whether a running horse has all its feet off the ground at the same time. The galloping sequence was made on a race track, using twelve cameras each equipped with an electro-magnetic shutter on a clockwork timing mechanism. In some respects Muybridge's experiments in movement, along with those of Marey, were the first steps towards the motion picture industry – Muybridge projected his action sequences with a fast shutter, and through his 'zoogyroscope' projector, which used a revolving disc.

Nanometre (nm)

One thousand millionth of a metre, a unit for measuring the wavelength of electromagnetic radiation. It is now replacing Ångstrom units in photographic contexts; one nanometre is equal to ten Ångstrom units.

Negative

Photographic image in which light tones are recorded as dark and dark tones as light. Lightwaves transmitted from the subject cause the SILVER HALIDES in the EMULSION to change through various tones of grey to black on subsequent development. The more intense the light the stronger the effect it has on the halides, and thus the darker they turn; areas from which little or no light is reflected leave clear areas on the emulsion – a reversal of the original scene. In colour negatives, every colour in the original subject is represented by its complementary. A positive image, corresponding in tonal values to the original subject, is made from a negative by passing a beam of light through it to a second light-sensitive material, usually printing paper.

Negative carrier

Frame for holding negatives or transparencies in an enlarger, positioned between the light source and the lens. Large- and medium-format flexible-base films may need sandwiching between cover glasses to keep the film flat, but smaller formats can be held in a glassless frame.

Negative lens see LENS

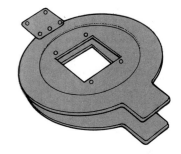

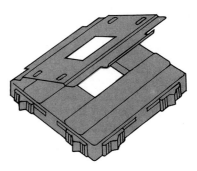

NEGATIVE CARRIERS

NIEPCE, JOSEPH NICEPHORE

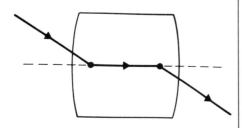

NODAL POINT

Neutral density filter see FILTER

Newton's rings
Narrow, multicoloured, concentric
bands that appear when two
transparent surfaces are sandwiched
together with imperfect contact. The
pattern is caused by INTERFERENCE,
when the minute gap between the two
surfaces is the same measurement as
the wavelength of reflected light. The
phenomenon sometimes occurs when
negatives are sandwiched between
glass plates in a negative carrier. Some
glass plates and slide mount glasses –
called 'Anti-Newton' – are very finely
etched in order to prevent the
appearance of Newton's rings.

Niepce de St. Victor, Claude Felix Abel
French cavalry officer, cousin of JOSEPH
NICEPHORE NIEPCE and inventor of the
albumen glass plate. This plate was
made by coating a glass with egg

whites whipped up with potassium
iodide. Left to harden, the plate was
later sensitized in a solution of silver
nitrate: the two chemicals reacted to
form light-sensitive silver iodide. After
exposure, the plate was developed in
gallic acid. Niepce de St. Victor's
inventive genius was considerable. He
devised a half-tone printing process
using bitumen-coated plates, and also
pre-empted GABRIEL LIPPMAN by taking
colour photographs on silver plates
employing the INTERFERENCE principle
of standing lightwaves.

Niepce, Joseph Nicephore
French amateur scientist and inventor
who holds the unique distinction of
creating the world's first photograph.
There are several worthy claimants to
the invention of photography,
including Thomas WEDGWOOD,
DAGUERRE, and FOX TALBOT. But it was
Niepce who produced in a CAMERA
OBSCURA, fitted with a lens, the first
actual photograph of a natural scene –
a view taken from a window of the
family home near Chalon-sur-Saône, in
1826. The picture itself, now in the
Gernsheim collection, measures
$8 \times 6\frac{1}{2}$in. It was made on a pewter plate
coated with bitumen of Judea, and
required an exposure time of
approximately eight hours. Bitumen
hardens when exposed to light in
proportion to the degree of exposure –
thus the highlights would harden
while the shadows remained soft and
soluble. These soluble areas were then
washed away with a mixture of
petroleum and oil of lavender, leaving
the hardened areas as a positive image.
The bitumen showed up as highlights,
while the revealed pewter plate under
the washed-away areas represented
the shadows. The picture remained
undiscovered for over sixty years, but
by a remarkable and painstaking piece
of detective work on the part of the
Gernsheims, was rediscovered in a
locked trunk, in an attic in Kew,
Surrey, England, in the 1950s.

Nodal point
Two points, front and rear, on the optical AXIS of a compound lens, used as references from which to make basic measurements such as focal length. Light entering a lens at a specific angle usually leaves at a different angle. However, there are two points on the axis such that a ray of light directed towards one appears to leave through the other in a parallel direction. These are the nodal points.

Nodark camera
A camera processing its own film, and manufactured in the 1890s. Called 'Nodark' (since darkroom processing was avoided) the makers ran into trouble with Kodak, who considered it too close an anagram of their own trade name, and issued a writ against the Nodark Company for infringement, whereon the name was withdrawn. The Nodark camera was by no means unique; FOX TALBOT had suggested a camera/darkroom combination, SCOTT ARCHER actually produced one, and during the following fifty years, quite a few different types were designed by independent inventors. True 'instant' photography had to wait for EDWIN LAND and the POLAROID CAMERA of 1947.

Nonsubstantive films
Colour reversal films that do not have colour-forming couplers incorporated in their emulsion, these being instead in the processing solutions. Kodachrome TRIPACKS are the only films of this type currently made.

Notches
Indentations cut in the edges of sheet film to indicate the emulsion side – if the notch is cut from the top left of the film when held vertically, the emulsion (matt side) is facing away from you. Notches of various shapes and sizes indicate different types of emulsion so that sheets of film can be identified even in total darkness.

Opacity
Light-stopping attribute of a material. The greater the opacity, as opposed to transparency, of a substance, the more light it will stop. In photography, opacity is expressed as a ratio of the amount of light falling on the surface of the material to the amount transmitted by it. A substance transmitting half the light falling on it has an opacity of 2, one transmitting a third of the light falling on it an opacity of 3, and so on.

Opal glass
White translucent glass, used mainly as a light diffuser in enlargers and as the viewing surface of light boxes.

Open-aperture metering
System of exposure metering, now almost universal on SLR cameras, in which the lens remains at its widest aperture until immediately prior to the moment of exposure, although by mechanical or electrical coupling the meter acknowledges whatever aperture has been set and reads accordingly. The advantage of this system over the older method of stop-down metering is that the viewing screen retains maximum brightness whatever aperture has been set, the diaphragm automatically closing to this aperture when the shutter release is pressed. In stop-down metering, the diaphragm has to be physically adjusted to the required aperture to obtain a correct reading. Although this means that the viewing screen progressively darkens as the aperture decreases in size, a compensating advantage is that it shows an approximation of the available depth of field.

Open flash
Technique of firing flash manually after the camera shutter has been opened, instead of synchronizing the flash automatically. A particular form of open flash – known as 'painting with light' – is a technique often used

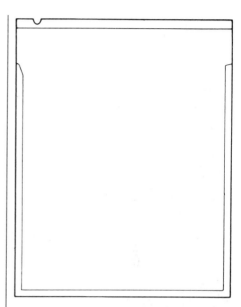

NOTCH

OPEN FLASH

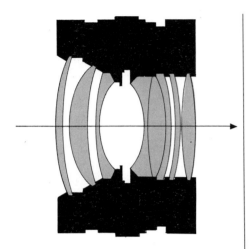

OPTICAL AXIS

when making long exposures in large dim interiors, the photographer firing off several flashes from different positions while the shutter is open.

Optical axis
Imaginary line through the centre of an optical system (for example a compound lens) at right angles to the image plane. Light passing through the lens along the optical AXIS is not refracted and is thus free of distortion.

Optical flat
High-quality element of optical glass with the two main surfaces polished to make them as flat and parallel as possible. Optical flats are used for filters when very great accuracy of performance is required.

Optical glass see also LENS
Glass of high quality and purity specially produced for the manufacture of lenses and other optical equipment. Optical glass must have precisely defined standards of dispersion and refraction, and therefore must be

physically and chemically as uniform as possible, free from bubbles and other deformities. It must also transmit the maximum amount of light and not selectively absorb light of different wavelengths. Durability – resistance to water vapour, atmospheric gases and so on – is also a desirable quality, but it is not always possible to combine this with the necessary optical properties. There are two main types of optical glass: flint glass, containing lead oxide, which has a high refractive index and high degree of dispersion; and crown glass, made with barium oxide, which combines a high refractive index with low dispersion.

Optical wedge
Device used in SENSITOMETRY, consisting of a wedge-shaped strip of material ranging from clear at one end to opaque at the other, either in regular steps (step wedge) or in a continuous transition (continuous wedge).

Orthochromatic
Term applied to black and white photographic emulsions sensitive to the blue and green regions of the spectrum but not to red or orange light. In the 19th century, all emulsions were either orthochromatic or 'ordinary' – that is, sensitive only to the blue region of the spectrum; the first PANCHROMATIC plates were introduced in the early years of the 20th century, stimulated by the work of chemists such as the Austrian BENNO HOMOLKA, who discovered the important red-sensitizing dye pinacyanol in 1904.

Ostwald system
System of colour classification invented by the German chemist Wilhelm Ostwald and published by him during World War I. Ostwald's system is somewhat similar to Munsell's, and arranges colours according to the amount of white, black and saturated colour they contain.

ORTHOCHROMATIC

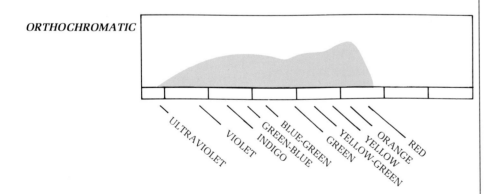

Overdevelopment

Over-long contact of emulsion with the developer, or use of a developing solution that is too powerful or too warm for the particular film. Overdevelopment, which results in very dense highlights and marked contrast, can be corrected to a certain extent by immersing the film in a reducing bath. For deliberate overdevelopment see PUSHING.

Overexposure

Excessive exposure of a photographic material to light. Overexposed negatives (colour or black and white) generally lack contrast and highlight detail; overexposed transparencies are 'thin' with burnt-out highlights. Acceptable prints can often be made from black and white negatives by using a hard grade of paper or by treating the negative with a reducing agent; acceptable colour prints from overexposed negatives may call for prolonged exposures and further adjustments to the filter pack. It is not possible totally to negate the effects of gross overexposure of transparencies.

Oxidation

Deterioration of chemical activity, for example in the developer exposed for a period to the air, and by action on SILVER HALIDES in photographic materials, i.e. the silver halides cause the developing agent to oxidize.

Ozobrome see MANLEY, T.

OVERDEVELOPMENT

OVEREXPOSURE

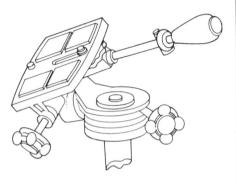

PAN AND TILT HEAD

PANORAMIC CAMERA

Pan-and-tilt head

Type of TRIPOD head employing independent locking mechanisms to allow movement in two planes at right angles to each other. Thus the camera can be locked in one plane while remaining free to move in the other. Movement in the horizontal plane is called pan, movement in the vertical plane tilt.

Panchromatic see also
ORTHOCHROMATIC
Term used to describe black and white photographic emulsions that are sensitive to all the visible colours (although not necessarily uniformly so). Panchromatic films owe their wide-spectrum sensitivity to various sensitizing dyes.

Panning see page 124

Panoramic camera see WIDE-ANGLE
CAMERA

Parallax
Apparent displacement of an object brought about by a change in viewpoint. In photography, the term parallax error is used to refer to the discrepancy between the image of a subject as viewed and as recorded on cameras in which the viewing lens is separate from the 'taking' lens and thus has a slightly different viewpoint (for example 35mm non-reflex cameras and twin-lens reflex cameras). With these cameras, parallax difference is generally apparent at subject distances closer than about six feet, when some form of compensation becomes necessary (the distance varies with the focal length of the lens being used). Non-reflex cameras often have lines in the viewfinder showing the allowance that has to be made, and some TLRs have a built-in compensation device in the form of a bar or blind (linked to the focusing controls) that moves across the focusing screen, showing the part of the image that will be cut off at various subject distances. Another method of overcoming parallax error with TLRs is, when the shot has been set up, to raise the camera by the distance between the two lenses. This can be done by simply measuring the distance and raising the tripod by this amount, or more accurately by using a special raising device that fits between the camera and the tripod. For precision close-ups, however, it is essential to use either a SINGLE-LENS REFLEX or LARGE-FORMAT CAMERA as they are parallax-free, the image on the

viewing screen being exactly the same as that which will be recorded on the film.

Pentaprism

Five-sided prism used as part of the viewing system of eye-level SLR cameras to provide a laterally correct, upright image in the viewfinder. In practice many pentaprisms have more than five sides – usually eight – the additional facets being due to unnecessary parts of the prism having been cut off to reduce bulk.

Permanence

Ability of a photographic image to resist fading through exposure to light or other deterioration caused by atmospheric chemicals. Permanence is determined initially by the effectiveness of the processing, and in colour photographs by the stability of the dyes in the emulsion layers. Development and fixing must be followed by thorough washing to remove, as far as possible, all traces of those residual silver compounds that could affect the image's appearance. HYPO, for example, if left in the image can decompose into silver sulphide, causing a bleached or sepia-coloured appearance, and most other fixing agents can react in a similar way. If prints are to be mounted, dry mounting is the best method with regard to permanence, because it does not introduce any potentially harmful chemicals to the back of the print, as do many glues. When processed and stored carefully (in dry, well-ventilated conditions, preferably in metal rather than wooden cabinets), black and white photographic materials will generally stay in good condition indefinitely. In the case of archive material such as microfilm of precious documents, however, more stringent environmental management is necessary, including control of temperature and relative humidity, and filtering of the air to cleanse it of acid gases. Colour images are less permanent than black and white ones, and are especially susceptible to direct sunlight, as can often be seen in the fading of colour prints displayed as advertisements in estate agents' windows or outside cinemas. To obtain maximum life expectancy, colour images should be stored in refrigerated conditions or as monochrome separation negatives which can subsequently be combined to recreate the colours. For archival storage, it is possible that colour videotapes will take over from actual dye images.

Perspective see page 126

Phenidone

Popular developing agent, produced by Ilford. Phenidone, which is more active than metol, is claimed not to cause many of the skin problems sometimes associated with processing chemicals.

Photo-cathode

Device consisting of a light-sensitive layer of such metallic substances as antimony or sodium on a glass or quartz base, which discharges electrons when exposed to a certain level of light. The electrons in the layer absorb photons and acquire their energy, which is discharged as a steady stream towards, for example, a photographic emulsion. Photo-cathodes are used in IMAGE INTENSIFIERS and in television cameras.

Photo-electric cell

Light-sensitive cell used in the circuit of an EXPOSURE METER.

Photoflood lamp

Type of filament lamp designed to be overrun to produce a more intense light than that from conventional tungsten lamps of the same wattage. Photofloods work at a temperature near the melting point of the filament, and have a COLOUR TEMPERATURE of about 3,400K.

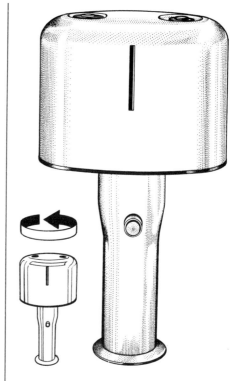

PANORAMIC CAMERA

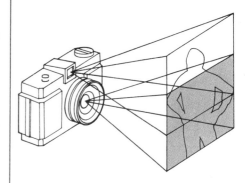

PARALLAX

Panning

The action of swinging the camera to follow a moving subject. Most often it is used to produce a sharp image of the subject against a blurred background, thus conveying a sense of movement. The celebrated French photographer Jacques-Henri Lartique was one of the first to use the panning technique – with a hand-held plate camera!

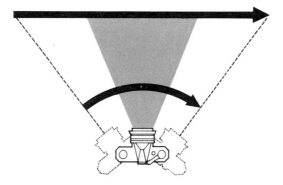

PANNING: The panning technique requires a little practise: let your camera follow the pace of the subject, shoot, then follow through smoothly without coming to an abrupt stop.

*Panning blurs the background and gives an impression of speed while the subject remains sharp, depending, of course on the shutter speed. In the **top** picture the camera is held in one position, and a slow shutter blurs the image of the car. In the second picture the car is frozen with a fast shutter. The shots **right** and **below right** show the effects of panning with a fast shutter.*

Perspective

Means by which the illusion of a three-dimensional object or space is created on a two-dimensional surface. The main elements of perspective in photography are diminution of size and convergence of lines with distance (linear perspective); the overlapping of forms; and the modifying effect of distance on colour known as AERIAL PERSPECTIVE. Depth can also be suggested by DIFFERENTIAL FOCUSING. Choice of viewpoint is a crucial factor in determining the perspective effect of a photograph, and choice of lens is also important, long-focus lenses appearing to 'compress' depth and wide-angle lenses having the opposite effect. Perspective effects can also to some extent be controlled (or intentionally distorted) by adjusting the relative positions of the lens and film. These CAMERA MOVEMENTS are normally possible only on large-format cameras, but on medium-format and 35mm cameras a limited range is made available by the use of a SHIFT LENS (sometimes known as a perspective control lens), which is used mainly in architectural photography.

Lenses of different focal lengths can affect perspective in a picture. With the camera in the same position, the pictures **left and below** show how perspective can be exaggerated with a wide-angle lens, and rendered increasingly shallow by increased focal length.

PHOTOGRAM

PHOTOMONTAGE

Photogram

Photographic image produced without a camera or lens by arranging objects on the surface of photographic film or paper, or so that they cast a shadow directly on to the material as it is being exposed. This was one of the earliest photographic techniques, used by THOMAS WEDGWOOD and FOX TALBOT, who made negative images of natural objects by direct contact on a photographic base (subjects such as plants can be kept flat with a sheet of glass). In its purest form, a photogram will have a solid black background with the shapes of the objects in white, but by varying such factors as the strength, direction and character of the light source, different (often unpredictable) effects can be obtained. Indeed, the scope for imaginative experimentation and abstract composition with this essentially simple technique is very considerable – the American artist Man Ray produced some particularly outstanding work in this field (he called his photograms 'rayographs'). It is also possible to produce colour photograms, using coloured paper and filters.

Photogrammetry

Branch of science concerned with using photographs to make accurate measurements. The use of aerial photographs in land surveying and map making is an example of photogrammetry, and photogrammetric techniques can also be used, for example, to measure the dimensions of buildings.

Photography

The science or art of producing pictures by the action of light upon prepared light-sensitive materials. As commonly understood, photography is the technique of producing pictures on film and on photographic printing paper through the agency of a CAMERA.

Photomacrography see page 130

Photometer

Instrument for measuring or comparing light intensity. An exposure meter is a kind of photometer, but generally the latter term is used for instruments that are employed, for example, to determine the levels of illumination in office buildings rather than for photographic purposes.

Photomicrography see also BRIGHT FIELD AND DARK FIELD and page 132

Photomontage

Technique of combining several prints or portions of prints into one image. Elements can be joined, overlapped or blended together to create patterns, panoramas or other images, and mounted on a flat surface.

pH value

Indication of the degree of acidity or alkalinity of a solution, strictly defined as the logarithm of the concentration of hydrogen ions in grams per litre. The scale of pH values, on which water is neutral at pH7, is as follows:

0–2	Strongly acid
3–4	Acid
5–6	Slightly acid
7	Neutral
8–9	Slightly alkaline
10–11	Alkaline
12–14	Strongly alkaline.

In photography, pH values are important mainly in connection with developing agents, which generally work most efficiently in an alkaline solution.

Physiogram

Photographic image of the pattern traced out by a light source attached to a moving object. As well as being used in photographic experiments, physiograms are useful in industry for examining the operation of machinery, and for time and motion studies. Simple physiograms are produced by attaching a light source, such as a pencil torch (flashlight), to a pendulum suspended from the ceiling or a frame. In a darkened room, with the camera's shutter kept open for a time exposure, the light will record its movement as patterned tracks of light. Tests will be needed to establish the correct exposure, especially if filters are used in colour work.

Pincushion distortion see ABERRATION

Pinhole camera

Camera where the lens is substituted by a card or thin metal disc, punctured in the centre by a very fine pin or needle hole. Through this hole light-waves will pass to form an image on the film. Pinhole images have a lack of definition and an overall softness, but the pinhole gives great depth of field and depth of focus: the 'lens' can be any distance from the film plane, although a short BACK FOCUS will enable you to use shorter exposures. You can obtain an acceptable image by making a pinhole camera out of a shoe box, or better still, a pinhole in place of the lens on an SLR camera. Take a disc of thin metal, slightly larger than the orifice of the lens mount and pierce it in the centre with a needle. Remove any burrs with fine emery paper, and tape down the disc to make a lightproof join. The subject must be brightly illuminated, when the image can actually be seen through the viewfinder. Focusing is not required, but you will need a tripod and cable release. With 100 ISO colour film, try bracketing around 1/8 second and 1/2 second, because exposure times may vary according to the diameter of the hole and the strength of the light.

Plate camera see LARGE-FORMAT CAMERA

PHOTOMONTAGE

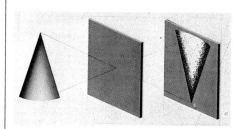

PINHOLE

Photomacrography

The production of photographic images at a scale of reproduction on the film of 1:1 (life-size) or larger. A more commonly used term for close-up work is MACROPHOTOGRAPHY, although this can also be used to refer to the production of giant photographs.

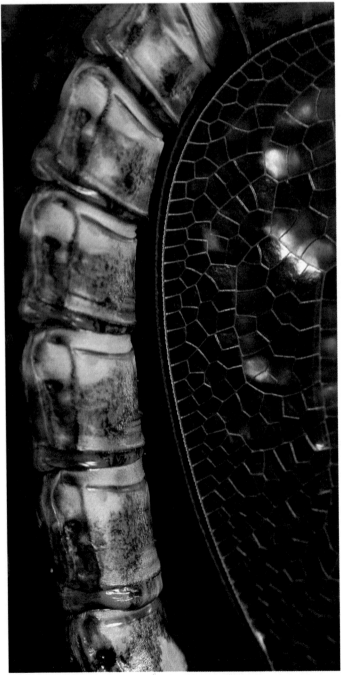

Photomicrography

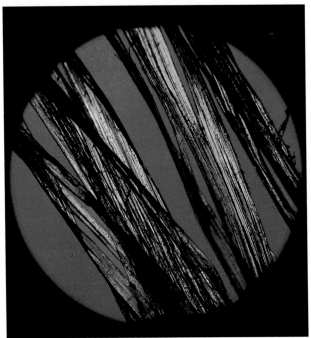

For magnifications greater than that achieved by a macro lens, a microscope with an adaptor for an SLR is required. TTL metering is the most suitable system for photomicrography so the SLR is ideal. To set up a shot, place the microscope slide on the stage, direct the light source on to the subject to illuminate it evently, and focus with the microscope controls. Select the widest camera aperture for maximum brightness and alter shutter speed to gain correct exposure. Among the best subjects for photomicrography are biological specimens such as tiny animals and plant – water fleas, house mites, diatoms. Use electronic flash fitted with a low-voltage tungsten lamp as a light source.

Left: Micro x 50 Polypropylene fibres under the polarizing microscope.
Below: Dermatophagodes Pteronissinus, house dust mite

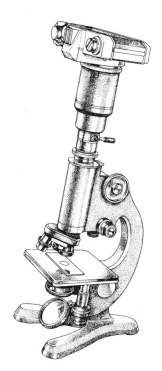

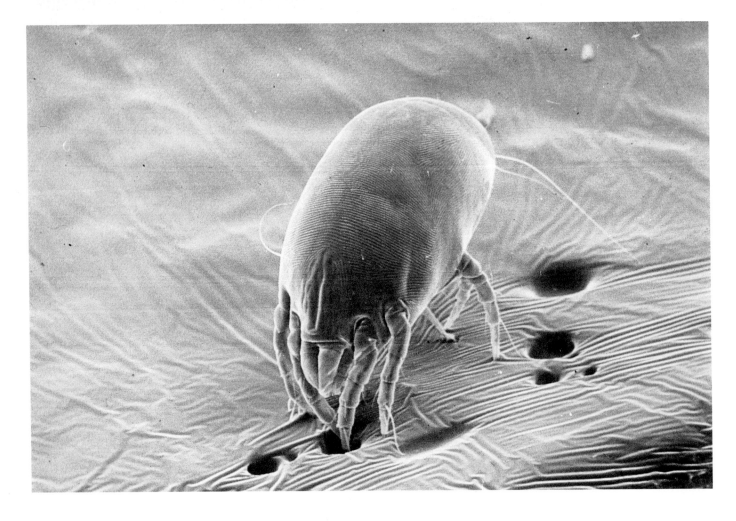

Technique of taking photographs through a microscope. SLR cameras are most suitable for use with microscopes because of their through-the-lens viewing and metering, the camera body being fitted to the microscope by means of a special adapter. Optical microscopes can magnify up to about × 2,000, but electron microscopes, which use a beam of electrons (negatively charged atomic particles) rather than light, can magnify up to × 1,000,000 or more. Electron microscopes usually have a special camera built in at the base of the equipment. A photograph taken through a microscope is correctly called a photomicrograph, sometimes abbreviated to micrograph. The term microphotography, which refers to the copying of documents and similar materials on to a very small format film, is often confused with photomicrography.

Silicon wafer ink taper hole for jet printer
Double exposure Micro x 125

Point-source lamp

Arc lamp used in enlargers and projectors. An arc current, conducted by mercury vapour between two tungsten filaments or beads, heats the tungsten, which becomes incandescent and emits a powerful concentrated light.

Polarized light

Light whose vibrations are confined to a single plane. Waves of light are usually unpolarized, having electrical and magnetic vibrations in every plane, but polarized light follows a simple and regular vibration pattern, a phenomenon that has various consequences and applications in optics and photography. Light (or part of it) may become polarized in several ways – for example, when it is reflected at certain angles from flat, polished, non-metallic surfaces such as glass, water or wooden furniture; when it is scattered by tiny particles of gas or dust in the atmosphere; and when it passes through certain translucent crystals. Man-made polarizing filters, in effect screens made up of many tiny polarizing crystals, can be used for various purposes in photography, notably darkening blue skies and eliminating unwanted reflections from non-metallic surfaces. When eliminating reflections, the polarizing filter is, in fact, blocking the light that has already been polarized and passing the non-polarized part. The filter is able to do this because it has a specific plane of polarization, and thus by rotating the filter the proportion of light inhibited can be varied. Further variation is possible with two polarizing filters, and if they are placed with their planes of polarization at right angles to each other, no light at all is passed (this phenomenon was first noticed by the 17th-century Dutch scientist Christiaan Huygens, who discovered that if the crystals of certain translucent minerals were placed with their long axes at right angles, they stopped the passage of light). Two polarizing filters can thus be used as a kind of variable neutral-density filter, and the two types of filter are, in fact, very similar in appearance. Polarizing filters used

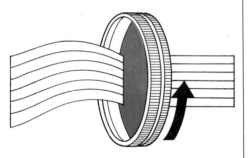

POLARIZING FILTER

POLAROID CAMERA

in pairs can be particularly useful in photomicrography; certain crystals, for example, may be indistinguishable in ordinary light, but differ in their abilty to polarize light and therefore show up clearly when the filters are suitably rotated. As well as being scientifically useful, this procedure can produce colour images of startling beauty.

Polaroid camera
Camera that produces more or less instantaneous pictures by using a 'sandwich' of film, processing chemicals and printing paper. After exposure the sandwich is ejected from the camera through rollers that rupture pods containing the chemicals. Development usually takes about 10 seconds to a minute. Although Polaroid cameras are most closely associated with family snapshots, Polaroid film has also become an invaluable aid to studio photography, as it enables lighting and exposure to be accurately monitored before a shot is made on ordinary film. Polaroid backs are available for almost all large- and medium-format cameras and also can be fitted to some 35mm SLRs. In addition, Polaroid markets a 'professional' camera, the 600SE, a 'press' type with interchangeable lenses, producing $4\frac{1}{4} \times 3\frac{1}{4}$in prints with an image area of about $3\frac{3}{4} \times 3$in. There are several types of Polaroid film, colour and black and white, and with one exception they produce only a print and not a negative, so additional prints can usually be made only by copying the original print to make a conventional negative. The exception is Type 665, a black and white film that produces a print and recoverable negative at the same time.

POP
Abbreviation for printing-out paper. Light-sensitive material that forms a visible image without development. Printing-out papers have a wide tonal range but a rather limited application.

Popping
Tendency for a negative or mounted transparency to buckle in the heat of a projector or enlarger, and go out of focus. This can be avoided by using a negative carrier or slide mount that holds the film but does not grip it tightly, allowing for some freedom of expansion.

Positive see NEGATIVE

Positive lens see LENS

Posterization see page 136

Power-winder see MOTOR-DRIVE

Preservative see DEVELOPER

Primary colours
In the ADDITIVE SYNTHESIS of colour, blue, green and red. Lights of these colours can be mixed together to give white light or light of any other colour.

Prime lens
Lens of fixed focal length either dedicated to one particular make of camera, or a lens by an independent maker that can be used with a certain type of camera. The standard lens, in an SLR, for example, is a prime lens. The term is also used to denote the element in a ZOOM lens assembly that does the most work to provide the optical power.

Prism
Optical glass or other transparent substance having polished surfaces designed to refract or reflect light at a specific angle depending upon the prism's design. In photography the prism most widely used is the PENTAPRISM in the SLR camera. This is typically a five-sided glass prism that conveys the image passing through the lens and reflected up from the mirror to the eyepiece so that the image is the right way up and not laterally reversed.

PRIMARY COLOURS

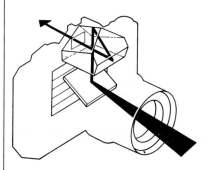

PRISM

Posterization

Technique of drastically simplifying the tones of an image by making several negatives from an original, with different degrees of density and contrast, and then sandwiching them together and printing them in register. The technique is so called because it makes it possible to produce, by using the high-contrast properties of lith film, the bold, striking effects associated with the style of posters during the 1930s in which shapes were filled in with solid, unshaded colours. Many different combinations are possible in posterization, and there is considerable scope for experimentation.

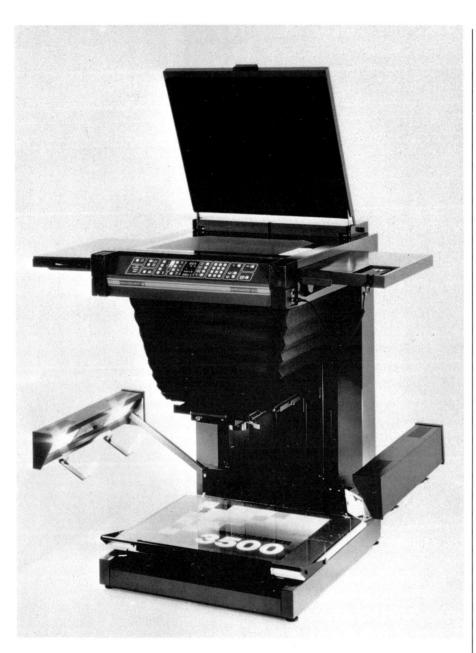

PROCESS CAMERA

very large (capable of making negatives over 4 feet square), with motor-driven movements enabling settings to be made with extreme accuracy. In the largest types, the end holding the film may be built in to a DARKROOM.

Process film
Slow, fine-grained film of good resolving power, used mainly for copying work.

Process lens
Highly corrected lens used for copying illustrations for subsequent photo-mechanical reproduction. As fast exposures are not needed in copying work, process lenses have fairly small maximum apertures (generally about f8 or f11), which gives the lens designer greater scope for achieving the high degree of correction needed. As well as being more accurately corrected than conventional camera lenses for the various types of spherical ABERRATIONS, process lenses are apochromatic (that is, corrected for three colours instead of the usual two), and consequently they are very expensive to manufacture.

Projector
Apparatus for throwing an image from a transparency on to a screen. Typically, the system employs a projector lamp (usually a tungsten filament type), a condenser, cooling fan, film carrier and lens. In addition, the projector may have a magazine for rapid loading and changing, and a means of remote control or preprogrammable operation. Many modern projectors also have an AUTOFOCUSING device that detects any flexing of the slide caused by heating and adjusts the focus to compensate for it. Most projectors are for transparencies in 2 × 2in mounts (they are usually 35mm slides, but medium-format 'superslides' – $1\frac{5}{8} \times 1\frac{5}{8}$in – also use this size mount).

Process camera
Special type of large-format camera used for extremely high-quality copying work, usually to make images for photomechancial reproduction or for scientific work. There are various different types of process cameras, some arranged horizontally, others vertically. The most specialized may be

Models are also made for the 110, 126 and $2\frac{1}{4} \times 2\frac{1}{4}$ formats, and some 35mm projectors are capable of accepting slides of smaller formats. Projectors are usually intended to be used in a darkened room, but there are some small, portable models with built-in screens that can be used in daylight.

Programmed exposure see
AUTOMATIC EXPOSURE

Protar lens
The first lens to bear the name 'ANASTIGMAT'. It was designed in 1890 by German optician Paul Rudolph of Zeiss, and consisted of two cemented elements, front and rear, with a stop between. The arrangement was partly based on the RAPID RECTILINEAR and on the ROSS CONCENTRIC, Rudolph having adapted and modified the front half of the Rapid Rectilinear lens (a divergent and convergent meniscus) with the rear half of the Ross (double concave and double convex). Constructed of the newly devised (1880s) Jena Crown and flint glasses, the arrangement corrected spherical aberration and astigmatism yet allowed an aperture of f8.

Pushing
Prolonging the development of film beyond the normal duration in order to compensate for underexposure or to increase CONTRAST. Pushing a film is often used after uprating (rating of a film at a higher speed index than that at which it was designed to be used), which in practical terms means underexposing to cope with low light conditions or to gain fast shutter speeds. An ASA 400 film uprated to ASA 800 represents one stop underexposure and is usually compensated for by increasing or 'pushing' the development time. It is a useful technique in, for example, photo-reportage or sports photography, when it may be necessary to work with weak available light.

Quarter-plate
Term used to describe a negative or (now more commonly) a print measuring $3\frac{1}{4} \times 4\frac{1}{4}$in.

Quartz-iodine lamp
Incandescent lamp with a quartz envelope containing a tungsten filament and a trace of iodine. The iodine vaporizes as the lamp gets hot and prevents the deposits of burning tungsten from collecting on the envelope. Instead, the tungsten-iodine vapour is deposited on the filament, thus recycling the tungsten. The process prolongs the life of the lamp, increasing its working efficiency and brightness. This type of lamp has now been largely replaced by the tungsten halogen lamp, in which bromine takes the place of iodine, and types of silica envelopes other than quartz are used.

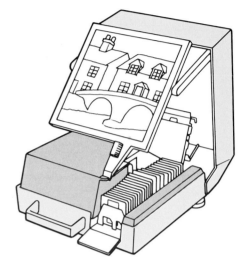

Screen projector for 35mm slides

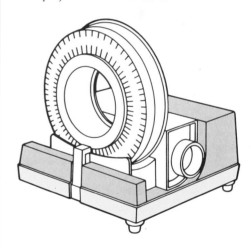

Magazine projector with circular magazine

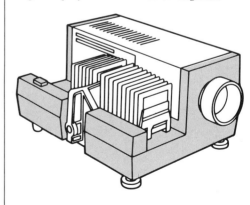

Simple slide projector with slide carrier
PROJECTORS

RACK AND PINION

Rack and pinion
Mechanism for focusing used on many large-format cameras. The focusing wheel is fixed to a pinion wheel that engages in a toothed rack along the baseboard of the camera. When the focusing wheel is turned, the lens panel slides along the baseboard.

Rangefinder see FOCUSING

Rapid rectilinear or 'R.R.' lens
Pre-astigmat, early and very popular lens consisting of two symmetric doublets with the stop between – a doublet is a pair of complementary glasses, typically a positive and negative meniscus, cemented together. Although they were inclined to suffer from spherical ABERRATION at the edges of the field, the lens could be used at around f8, while some, such as Voigtlander's 1877 'Euryscope' lenses, operated at f6. The R.R. lens was also made as a wide-angle combination with a stop of f16. The best rapid rectilinears were made by Dallmeyer, and were relatively inexpensive when compared to the later anastigmats, but were really only suitable for landscape and architectural photography.

Reade, Reverend Joseph Bancroft
English clergyman, amateur scientist and independent inventor of a negative/positive process. Reade was the first to use, in 1837, hypo as a fixing agent (although the possibility had been suggested by HERSCHEL) and the first to use gallic acid as an accelerator, yet had failed to grasp that gallic acid was also a DEVELOPER. It would have been, as Reade himself put it, 'a feather in his cap', instead of which it fell to FOX TALBOT to note the significance of latent image development by gallic acid. Later, Fox Talbot was to patent Reade's discovery, and not without some acrimony on both sides. Even so, Reade's achievements were considerable: he had made an exposure, developed it, and fixed it with hypo. He had made photographs in the camera, negative and positive prints. He had even succeeded in taking a photograph of a person – the first such image ever made. But although Reade had exhibited his pictures, he neglected to publish the results of his experiments. He remains, though, one of the unsung heroes of early photography.

Ready light
Small neon indicator lamp on the housing of an ELECTRONIC FLASH UNIT. The light comes on when the unit's capacitors are fully charged, indicating that the flash is ready for use.

Real image
Visual image produced by a positive lens and one that can be focused on to a screen or film. The image passing through the lens of a camera on to the film plane is a 'real' image, as opposed to a 'virtual' image created by a negative lens. A positive lens causes lightwaves passing through it to converge, while a negative lens causes lightwaves to diverge, as in spectacle lenses, and gives a virtual image.

Reciprocity law
Principle according to which the density of the image formed when an emulsion is developed is directly proportional to the duration of the exposure and the intensity of the light. However, with extremely short or long exposures and with unusual light intensities the principle ceases to be valid and unpredictable results occur – this is known as reciprocity law failure. In colour photography it may cause colour casts, which to some extent can be compensated for with filters when the characteristics of the film are known.

Red-eye see page 142

Reducer
Chemical agent used to remove silver from a negative or print, thereby reducing its density. Confusion often arises between the terms 'reducer' and 'reducing agent'; the latter refers to a chemical agent used to convert the exposed SILVER HALIDES in an emulsion to metallic silver, and is therefore a synonym for DEVELOPER.

Reflector
Any surface capable of reflecting light, but in photography generally understood to mean sheets of white or silvered card employed to reflect light into shadow areas. Lamp reflectors are generally dish-shaped mirrors, the lamp recessed into the concave interior, which points towards the subject. Studio electronic flash equipment is often combined with an umbrella reflector, usually silvered, mounted on a stand.

Reflex camera
Generic name for types of camera employing a mirror in the viewing system to reflect the image on to a screen. There are two main types. The single-lens reflex (SLR) camera reflects the image to the screen by means of a hinged mirror that flips out of the light path when the film is being exposed. Viewing and taking functions are thus combined in one lens, and if the viewing system also employs a PENTAPRISM, the viewfinder shows exactly the same image as that which will be recorded on the film. The twin-lens reflex (TLR) has separate viewing and taking lenses of identical focal length. The upper (viewing) lens has a mirror behind it that reflects light to the focusing screen. At close subject distances, the difference of viewpoint between the two lenses causes PARALLAX ERROR. TLRs are now made only for medium-format film; SLRs are most popular in the 35mm format, but there are several high-quality medium-format SLRs.

Refraction see also ABERRATION, LENS and OPTICAL GLASS
The bending of lightwaves as they travel from one medium to another of different optical DENSITY. Three factors affect the degree of bending: the WAVELENGTH of the light; the composition of the second medium; and the angle at which the light enters it. The angle that the arriving wave makes with a line at right angles to the surface of the second medium is known as the angle of incidence; the angle that the light travelling through the medium makes with this line is known as the angle of refraction. Rays of light perpendicular to the INTERFACE between the two media are not subject to refraction. The amount of bending a medium produces is described numerically as its refractive index. Different colours of light (because they have different wavelengths) are refracted to different degrees, a phenomenon called DISPERSION.

Rehalogenization
The process of converting deposits of black metallic silver into SILVER HALIDES. The process may be used TO BLEACH prints in preparation for toning.

Relative aperture see APERTURE

Remote release
Cordless remote control device for firing the SHUTTER. Some such shutter control systems are sonic, some infrared using a miniature transmitter, a receiver mounted on the camera and a photo-resistor. In more advanced types the camera can be operated over considerable distances, for nature photography and surveillance work.

Replenishment
The regeneration of processing solutions by the addition of those chemicals that have become weakened or used up.

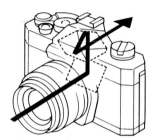

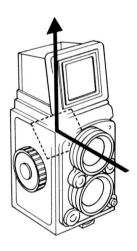

REFLEX CAMERA: The reflex system that conveys an image via an angled mirror is older than photography – it was invented for the CAMERA OBSCURA. Above, the SLR, below, the TLR.

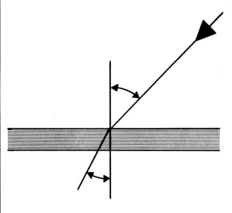

REFRACTION

Red eye

Effect seen in colour photographs when the flash is too close to the camera lens, and nearly level with the sitter's eyes. The unnatural, glowing red of the eyes is due to internal reflections from the vascular membrane behind the retina, which is rich in blood vessels. In black and white photography the phenomenon produces unusually light pupils. Red-eye can be avoided by making sure the subject is not looking directly at the camera or by using off-camera or BOUNCED FLASH.

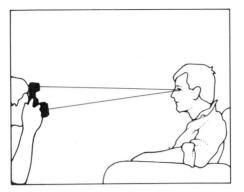 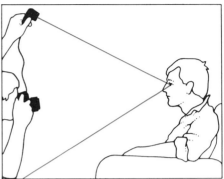

Resin-coated (RC) paper

Photographic printing paper coated with synthetic resin to prevent the paper base absorbing liquids during processing. RC papers can be processed more quickly than conventional papers as they require less washing and dry more quickly. In addition, RC papers do not require glazing. Against these obvious advantages of speed and convenience must be set the disadvantages that RC paper is easily scratched (especially when wet) and difficult to retouch successfully; some critics also suggest that the blacks it produces are somewhat lacking in depth compared to those obtained using conventional bromide paper.

Resolving power

Ability of an optical system to distinguish between elements that are very close together. The resolving power of a lens (expressed in lines per millimetre) is measured by using a special test chart consisting of a complex pattern made up of lines of varying thickness. An emulsion can also be said to have a resolving power, and if this is less than that of the lens used with it, some sharpness will be

RETOUCHING: Basic retouching can be carried out with limited equipment – two fine brushes, a ceramic palette, and retouching pigments. This is straightforward spotting, where marks can be corrected and blemishes eliminated.

lost. Factors other than resolving power also affect sharpness (see LENS).

Restrainer see DEVELOPER

Reticulation
Fine, irregular pattern appearing on the surface of an emulsion that has been subjected to a sudden and severe change in temperature or in the relative acidity/alkalinity of the processing solutions. The phenomenon is caused by the swelling and cracking of the gelatin emulsion and cannot be rectified once it has occurred. Reticulation may, however, give interesting effects to the final print when it is enlarged, and can be used as a means of experimenting with negatives that might otherwise be discarded.

Retouching
Handwork (on negatives, prints or transparencies) using a brush, AIRBRUSH, pencil or knife, together with specially prepared spotting and retouching fluids, to remove or disguise flaws or otherwise improve or alter the image. Retouching is usually carried out on prints rather than on negatives or transparencies because of the larger image area and the fact that mistakes can be more easily rectified. Large negatives can be retouched successfully, but the job requires considerable skill and experience.

Retrofocus
An arrangement of lens elements found mainly in wide-angle lenses. Wide-angle lenses have a very short focal length and the rear lens element must be close to the film plane to give the required angle of view. This arrangement is impractical with SLR cameras, since the camera design has to incorporate an angled mirror between the lens and the film plane. The gap between the rear element and the film plane is called the 'back focal distance', and it is the aim of the lens designer to allow a generous back focal distance for a short-focal-length lens. This is achieved by placing a negative lens in front of a positive lens, an arrangement also known as 'inverted telephoto' design since the TELEPHOTO system uses a positive front element and negative rear element. The nature of a positive lens is to convey and focus the image by converging the lightwaves; a negative lens diverges them, and careful choice of both negative and positive elements allows designers to lengthen or shorten the back focus.

Reversal film
Film that produces a positive image after one exposure and after processing. This is called reversal film since it reverses the negative image familiar with print film. The image layers in the tripack slide film produce a black positive linked to subtractive dyes, magenta, cyan and yellow. The black silver positive is bleached away leaving only a positive colour image in three superimposed dye layers.

Reversing ring
Device for attaching a lens to the camera body (or extension bellows) back to front. This helps to maintain good definition in close-up work.

Rim lighting see page 146

Ring flash see FLASH

Rising front
Movable lens panel that allows the lens to be moved vertically in a plane parallel to the film. It is the most commonly used CAMERA MOVEMENT, and is associated particularly with architectural photography: raising the lens panel enables the top of tall buildings to be included in the picture without distorting the vertical lines. On 35mm and medium-format cameras, a SHIFT AND TILT LENS performs a similar function.

RING FLASH

Rim lighting

Lighting arrangement, principally used in portraiture, in which the light comes from behind or above the subject, creating a bright rim of light around the contours.

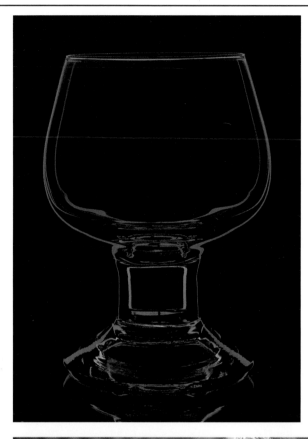

S

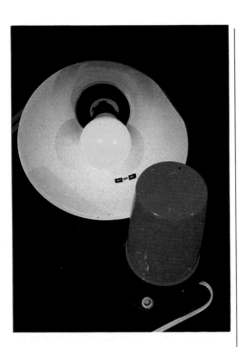

SAFELIGHT: A red safelight is best for all types of darkroom work – provided that there is no leakage of white light. For a temporary darkroom, red safelight bulbs are adequate, but for regular work a purpose-built safelight is a worthwhile investment.

Roll-film see FILM

Ross, Andrew
English optician and lens maker who supplied FOX TALBOT with the lenses for his cameras and made the lenses for BREWSTER's first stereoscope in 1851. These were achromatic (see ABERRATION) lenses of two elements in one combination. Ross also designed the first portrait lens in 1841, a combination of double front and rear elements. The most successful Ross lens was the concentric of 1888, made with Jena glass, designed with plano-concave and plano-convex doublets. It was the first ANASTIGMAT but the drawback was its small aperture – f16.

Russell, Colonel Charles see also DEVELOPMENT
Inventor of tannin dry plates and of alkaline pyrogallol developer. Col. Russell was an English amateur photographer who discovered the property of tannin to maintain the sensitivity of collodion dry plates – photographic plates in the 19th century were susceptible to spoilage through fermentation and other factors. His experiments with tannin led to a more significant discovery, viz., chemical DEVELOPMENT. Russell introduced the first practical process of alkaline development, by adding the ALKALI ammonia to the then widely used pyrogallic acid developer. The new formula was ahead of its time: alkaline development was 'chemical' as opposed to acid's 'physical' development, and later became an important feature in the gelatin-silver bromide dry plate. Where acid physical development coats the exposed SILVER HALIDES in the emulsion with additional silver added in the developer, and in effect 'silver plates' them, chemical development of the alkaline type chemically converts the exposed halides to metallic silver, a more powerful yet subtle process.

Sabattier effect
The partial reversal of the tones of a photographic image, resulting from a secondary exposure to light during DEVELOPMENT. Sometimes known as pseudo-solarization, it can be used to give interesting printing effects. The secondary exposure reverses the shadow areas of the negative, but only partially, because these dense areas have already become desensitized by chemical action during development; the resulting image is a mixture between a negative and a positive. See SOLARIZATION.

Safelight
Special darkroom lamp whose light is of a colour (such as red or orange) to which sensitized materials will not respond. Not all materials can be handled under a safelight, and some require a particular type designed specially for them. Some safelights have provision for change of filter colour, the filters being made of GELATIN or glass sheet. No safelight is entirely safe, however, since filters cannot block all critical WAVELENGTHS completely. Fogging will occur if the work is too close to the light, three feet away being judged the minimum safe distance. A lamp of a higher wattage than usual (25W is the normal maximum) can be used if the safelight is bounced off the darkroom ceiling, but tests for fog should be made before printing begins. Specialized safelights utilizing monochromatic sodium vapour lamps provide very bright working conditions, with minimal risk of fog.

Sandwiching
The projection or printing of two or more negatives or slides together to produce a composite image. Pictures of considerable complexity and visual impact can be produced by the sandwiching technique, which is widely employed in advertising and magazine editorial pictures.

Sanger Shepherd, Edward

English camera designer and manufacturer, and specialist in colour cameras, stereoscopic cameras, and colour processes, notably Sanger-Shepherd's CARBON PROCESS and imbibition print process of 1899 and 1906. The Sanger-Shepherd colour camera of 1907 needed but one exposure to make three negatives on one plate, through a beam-splitting prism and filters in front of the plate. An enthusiastic inventor, Sanger Shepherd's camera works 'put upon the market every requisite for working in colour'.

Saturated colour

Pure colour free from any admixture of grey. A saturated colour reflects light of only one or two of the three PRIMARY COLOURS; the addition of a third colour would desaturate it towards white, grey or black.

Saturated solution

Solution in such a condition that no more soluble substance can be dissolved in it at a given temperature.

Sayce and Bolton

Mid-19th century English photographers working in Liverpool whose names are linked by their revolutionary invention – photographic EMULSION for coating plates. Sayce alone was responsible for the idea, but Bolton made a significant, later contribution. The invention of emulsions rid photographers of the messy and lengthy COLLODION PROCESS. Briefly, wet plates had to be exposed while wet because the silver salts employed (silver nitrate) lost their sensitivity and crystallized when dried, and this affected the image. Sayce tried dissolving the nitrate in alcohol and mixing it in collodion charged with potassium bromide in place of the usual iodide, producing silver bromide in suspension. This was left to 'ripen' for 24 hours, which increased its

sensitivity. The emulsion could then be poured on a plate and left to dry, having first been preserved with tannin (see C. RUSSELL). Theirs was the first workable dry plate but the emulsion still contained an excess of silver salt. Bolton improved the product, manufactured by their Liverpool Dry Plate and Photographic Company, by washing the emulsion free of residual salts, and drying it to form a reconstitutable pellicle (see RICHARD KENNETT).

Scheele, Carl Wilhelm

Eighteenth-century Swedish chemist and early experimenter in the effects of light on silver salts. He confirmed Schulze's observation on the ACTINIC effect of light on silver chloride and in particular the rays at the violet end of the SPECTRUM. Scheele also observed the fixing properties of ammonia on silver chloride.

SANDWICHING

SCHÉELE

1742 - 1786

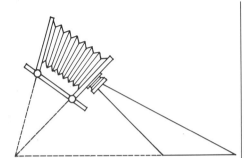

SCHEIMPFLUG PRINCIPLE: *Large format cameras with special movements can exploit depth of field by applying this optical principle – see CAMERA MOVEMENTS.*

SCHULZE JOHANN

Scheimpflug principle

Principle stating that for a large-format camera maximum DEPTH OF FIELD over the subject plane is obtained when the subject plane, lens plane and image plane are so inclined that if extrapolated they would meet at a common point. It is chiefly used to work out the optimum camera position to achieve overall sharpness when a subject is disposed in a plane inclined to the camera axis, but can also be used when the baseboard is tilted in enlarging, if the enlarger's negative plane can also be inclined.

Scheiner

A speed rating system for film emulsions devised by Julius Scheiner and used in Germany until replaced by the DIN scale. Though now obsolete it is still found on some old cameras, and like the DIN system is logarithmic rather than arithmetic.

Schinzel, Carl

Austrian scientist and the first experimenter in colour processes to propose the idea of the colour tripack, the idea subsequently developed by RUDOLPH FISCHER and MANNES AND GODOWSKY. Schinzel suggested a SUBTRACTIVE SYNTHESIS tripack where three superimposed emulsion layers could be mounted on one base to produce three SILVER HALIDE images, linked to dye molecules. The halide images would then be BLEACHED out leaving a colour positive. This was called by Schinzel his 'Katachromie' process of 1905. Unfortunately the tripack failed in practice since the bleach employed – hydrogen peroxide – also randomly bleached the dyes. Nevertheless it was a revolutionary idea and to Schinzel must be accorded the invention of the colour film used today.

Schlieren photography

Branch of scientific photography employing an optical system sensitive to, and capable of recording, small local differences in the refractive index of transparent media. As hot air has a different refractive index from cold air, Schlieren photography can record air movement that is invisible to the eye, and can be used to study, for example, airflow in windtunnels or the transfer of heat energy from living organisms to the atmosphere. Schlieren photography was first demonstrated in Germany in the 1860s, and 'Schlieren' is German for streaks or striations. As with many other branches of scientific photography, Schlieren photography can produce very striking and beautiful images.

Schulze, Johann Heinrich

German scientist who discovered, in 1725, the action of light upon silver nitrate. Schulze, though aware of the importance of his discovery that light could cause a chemical reaction, did not experiment far enough to pursue the phenomenon in a photographic sense, although he did produce a few stencils using a liquid precipitate of chalk and silver salts.

Scratch-proofing

Technique for hardening a photographic emulsion to protect it from abrasions. Hardness such as potassium or chrome alum can be contained in the fixing bath, but more durable and scratch-resistant finishes can be obtained using a solution of tannic acid and formalin.

Screen

Flat surface for receiving a projected photographic image. Screens are usually made of a matt white or glass beaded material such as fabric or plastic, and designed to be portable, although a white wall can of course serve as a screen.

Secondary colours

Colours resulting from mixing together any two of the primary colours, red, green or blue. The principal secondary colours used in colour film and printing processes are cyan (blue-green), magenta (red-blue) and yellow (red-green) and these colours are sometimes called the 'subtractive primaries'. The purity of these colours depends on their being produced by mixed coloured lights, and not pigments; red and green paints when mixed will not produce yellow, but grey, owing to the absorption of specific wavelengths of light by the pigment itself.

Selenium cell

Photocell used in some hand-held exposure meters, such as the Weston meter. Selenium cells work independently of batteries, and are marginally less sensitive than the battery-powered CdS and SPD cells, in low light levels. The cell generates an electric current when exposed to light, in proportion to the intensity of the light falling upon it. The fluctuations of current can thus be scaled to form a set of exposure calculations. Selenium cells need a fairly large light-receptive surface to function properly, which is why they are not used for TTL meters.

Self-timer

Mechanism employed in the majority of cameras to enable the shutter to be operated by delayed action. Useful for self-portraiture and to include the photographer in a group picture, and for helping to eliminate vibration in time exposures.

Sensitized material

Any support or base, such as paper, glass plates or film, bearing a coating of light-sensitive photographic EMULSION.

Sensitometry

Branch of science devoted to measuring the response of photographic materials to radiant energy and thereby establishing numerical values for the relationship between EXPOSURE and DENSITY. The most commonly used of these numerical values are FILM SPEEDS.

Separation negative

Black and white negative or, more usually, TRANSPARENCY made from a coloured image re-photographed through one of several coloured filters so as to record only one colour component of the original. For photomechanical printing, a set of three separation negatives recording the blue, green and red components are commonly obtained, together with a negative recording the tones of the image. These are used to make four printing plates to reproduce in shades of cyan, magenta, yellow and black. In theory, full-colour printing could be done with only three plates, but without a black plate a printed picture would lack punch: a solid black area would look like very dark brown. In books illustrated with colour pictures, the black plate usually carries also the textual matter. Very high-quality colour printing, as used, for example, in producing facsimiles of medieval manuscripts, may require the use of more than four plates to achieve maximum fidelity to the original.

Shade

Alternative term for a LENS HOOD.

Shading see DODGING

Sheet film

Individual pieces of film for use in large-format cameras. Sheet film, also known as cut film or flat film, is available in various sizes up to a normal maximum of 10×8in and is stored in DARK SLIDES.

Shellac Natural resin used for varnishing negatives and as an adhesive for DRY MOUNTING. It has now been generally superseded by synthetic resins.

SELF TIMER

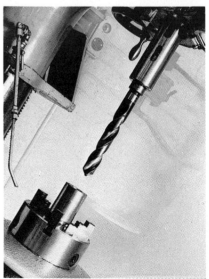

SHADING

Shift lens

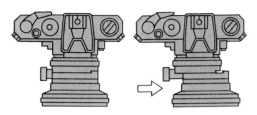

Lens for a 35mm or medium-format camera that can be moved off its axis to provide an equivalent for some of the CAMERA MOVEMENTS of large-format cameras. Also known as perspective control lenses, shift lenses can move both laterally and vertically (depending on the design, it may or may not be possible to use lateral and vertical movement at the same time) and are used chiefly in architectural photography to enable, for example, the top of a tall building to be included in the picture without tipping the camera backwards and thereby causing the vertical lines to converge. (The name shift lens is therefore somewhat paradoxical as 'shift' is the term used for lateral movement produced by a cross front on large-format cameras, whereas the camera movement used most in architectural photography is the rising front.) A shift lens made by Canon also incorporates a mechanism for moving it so that it is not parallel to the film plane, giving it a limited degree of the large-format camera's swing front and tilt movement. The focal length of shift lenses for 35mm cameras is either 28 or 35mm and maximum aperture ranges from f2.8 to f4. Although they share certain optical and mechanical characterisitcs (the diaphragm, for example, has to be operated manually so OPEN-APERTURE METERING is not possible), the shift lenses marketed by different manufacturers are surprisingly different in appearance and construction for instruments designed to perform the same task. For example, Pentax's 28mm f3.5 shift lens, which has built-in filters, is constructed of 12 elements in 11 groups; it is almost twice as long and three times as heavy as the Schneider PA Curtagon 35mm f4 shift lens, which is constructed of 7 elements in 3 groups.

Shutter

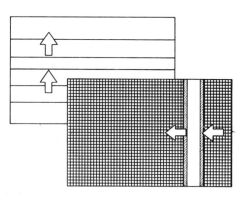

*An integral lens leaf shutter, **left**, and vertical and horizontal focal plane shutters, **above**.*

Mechanical device used to expose film to light for an exact period of time. There are two main types: between-the-lens shutters (sometimes called leaf shutters) and focal plane shutters. A between-the-lens shutter is built into the lens barrel, close to the diaphragm, and consists of thin metal blades or leaves that spring open when the camera is fired and close again when the time for which it has been set has elapsed. A focal plane shutter is built into the camera body, slightly in front of the focal plane, and consists of a system of cloth or metal blinds that travel across the image area either vertically or horizontally when the camera is fired, forming a slit that, according to its width and speed of travel, determines the length of the exposure. Both types of shutter have advantages and disadvantages. Focal plane shutters seal off the film between exposures while permitting light to pass through the lens, so they are used particularly in single-lens reflex cameras. The sealing-off of the film means that lenses can be changed at any time. Between-the-lens shutters are more expensive (and every lens has to have its own shutter), but they are quiet, smooth-working and more mechanically reliable than focal plane shutters. The fact that the between-the-lens shutter exposes the whole film frame at once gives it certain advantages over the focal plane shutter when using flash and when photographing fast movement. Between-the-lens shutters can be sychronized with flash at any speed, but focal plane shutters can generally be synchronized at only one fairly slow speed (usually 1/60 or 1/125) because the shutter has to be fully open to make sure the blinds do not cut off part of the image at the edges of the frame. When photographing fast motion, the position of the subject will have changed slightly by the time the shutter has completed its traverse of the film plane, and depending on the direction of movement of the subject and the shutter, various kinds of distortion can result. Between-the-lens shutters generally have a maximum speed of 1/500, focal plane shutters of 1/1000, 1/2000 or 1/4000. Faster speeds are obtainable with special shutters, and those used in scientific work, such as the Kerr cell, may be capable of exposures of less than one-millionth of a second. In the Kerr cell, two polarizing filters are placed on opposite sides of a glass tank containing nitrobenzine. A beam of light passes through the first filter, then through the tank, but is stopped by the second filter, set in a different plane of polarization. When an electric current is passed through the nitrobenzine, it has the effect of rotating the plane of polarization, allowing the light beam to pass through the second filter and on to the emulsion. The speed of the Kerr cell shutter thus depends on the duration of the current, which is discharged as a pulse from a condenser or capacitor. Using a high-frequency oscillating electric field, a Kerr cell shutter can be opened and shut millions of times a second.

SLOW SHUTTER

FAST SHUTTER

Shutter priority see AUTOMATIC EXPOSURE

Shutter releases
Remote control device for firing the shutter, the simplest of which is the CABLE RELEASE which screws in to the shutter button on the camera. Most have a lock that allows you to operate the B SETTING to keep the shutter open for long exposures. Other releases include pneumatically operated bulb releases (one of the earliest forms of shutter operation) consisting of the plunger, a fine rubber hose and rubber bulb. Some shutter control systems are sonic, some infrared using a miniature transmitter, a receiver mounted on the camera to work by radio control, and by a photo-resistor. In more advanced types the camera can be operated over considerable distances, for nature photography and surveillance work.

Silica gel
Moisture-absorbing material and a form of silicon dioxide. Packets of granular silica gel help to prevent moisture condensing inside cameras and camera lenses.

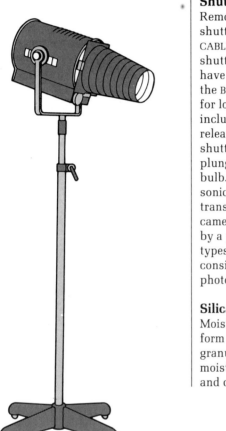

SNOOT

SPECTRUM

Silicon Photo Diode (SPD) see also EXPOSURE METERS
Photocell used in hand-held exposure meters and in cameras. They are highly sensitive to low light levels and have rapid response to light changes making them ideal for use in TTL meters.

Silver halide
Chemical compound of silver with a HALOGEN (for example, silver iodide, silver bromide or silver chloride). Silver bromide is the principal light-sensitive constituent of modern photographic EMULSION, though other silver halides are also used. The latent image produced on these compounds by the action of light is converted to metallic silver by developers.

Skylight filter see FILTER

Slave unit see FLASH

SLR see page 158

Snoot
Conical lamp attachment used to control the beam of a studio light.

Soft box
Lightweight frame, usually with a covering of cloth or some other material, for enclosing a studio light. The front of the box has a white diffuser for softening the flash or tungsten source.

Soft focus see page 160

'Soho' camera
Type of plate camera made by a number of British firms circa 1910, and most successfully by Marions of Soho, from which the camera acquired its generic title. The design included an improved mirror/shutter mechanism with a retractable hinge and a pneumatic operation that eliminated vibration.

Solarization see page 162

Spectrum

Term used to refer either to the whole range of electromagnetic radiation or to the part of it that is detected by the human eye as light (the visible spectrum). All electromagnetic radiation is pure energy, but the various types of radiation have different WAVELENGTHS; at one end of the spectrum, radio waves have relatively long wavelengths, and at the other end, gamma rays have extremely short (intense) wavelengths and can be dangerous. Each part of the spectrum can be resolved, received or detected by apparatus such as wireless equipment and geiger counters, and each has its industrial and scientific uses. The band of the spectrum visible to the human eye is very narrow (though some animals, such as certain species of snakes, can see infrared as well, and some insects, notably bees, can see ultraviolet). It can be resolved into its constituent colours by a prism, which breaks it into bands of red, orange, yellow, green, blue, indigo and violet. Some other wavelengths, notably infrared, ultraviolet, X-rays and gamma rays, can be recorded by special photosensitive materials.

Specular reflection

Reflection of light from a smooth surface, when every ray is reflected at the same angle. Irregular surfaces produce diffuse reflection (see DIFFUSION), which has the effect of softening light.

Speed

Term used in photography to refer to (1) the degree of sensitivity to light of a film emulsion (see FILM SPEED) or (2) the maximum aperture of a lens (see APERTURE).

Speed Graphic

Famous American press camera, affectionately called the 'Speed G' and designed by William Folmer of the Folmer & Schwing Division of Eastman Kodak (who also made the press Graflex camera of 1898) in 1912. Made in $2\frac{1}{4} \times 3\frac{1}{4}$in and in 5×7in formats the Speed Graphic had a focal plane shutter, a coupled rangefinder and flash synchronization. Updated versions of the camera were still in use in the 1950s.

Spherical aberration see ABERRATION

Spotlight

Lamp unit designed to emit a concentrated beam of light. Spotlights have clear lamps and polished reflectors (usually a hemispherical concave mirror), and are often fitted with a FRESNEL LENS, which by its design is lightweight and heat-resistant, and throws a beam of evenly directed light. Many spotlights are also fitted with grooved guides to hold BARN DOORS, FILTERS and SNOOTS that help to direct, shape, colour or diffuse the light beam.

Spot meter see EXPOSURE METER

Spotting

Retouching a print or negative to remove spots and blemishes.

Sprocket holes

Regular, rectangular perforations along the edge of 35mm and other films that engage the teeth of the camera's wind-on mechanism.

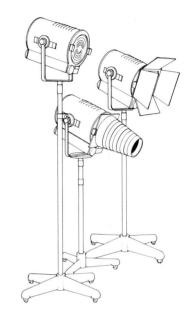

SPOTLIGHT

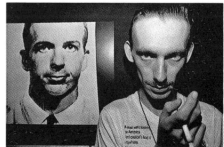

SPOTTING: Before and after.

SLR

Common and much used abbreviation for the Single Lens Reflex camera where the image passes through the lens, via an angled mirror and PENTAPRISM to the eyepiece. The reflex system is older than photography, since mirrors were used in the camera obscura. The first innovator to apply the reflex mirror to the modern camera was Thomas Sutton, in 1861 (the year in which W. ENGLAND patented the focal plane shutter). The first auto-reflex was patented by S. D. McKellen in 1888, but the addition of a pentaprism had to wait until 1949 and the arrival of the Contax S.

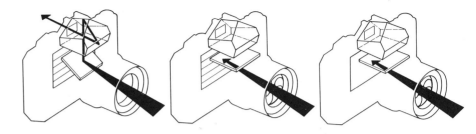

The light path, transmitted by the lens, strikes a hinged mirror set at an angle of 45° and travels through a pentaprism to the viewing screen and eyepiece, presenting the image the right way up and right way *round. On triggering the shutter, the mirror flips up to allow the image to strike the film at the focal plane, then returns ready for the next exposure.*

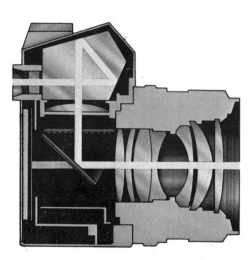

The 35mm SLR system

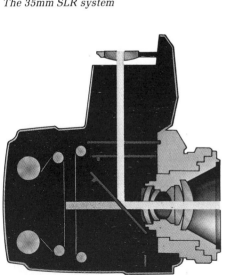

The medium format conveys the image directly to a top mounted screen.

Soft focus

Deliberately diffused or blurred definition of an image. Soft focus effects, used most typically in portraiture to create a dreamy, romantic image and to hide blemishes, can be achieved on the camera or during enlarging. Special lenses or filters can be used to soften the image by diffusing the light or giving a controlled degree of spherical ABERRATION (several manufacturers make lenses in which the degree of aberration and thus of softness can be continuously varied to a certain point). Similar effects can be obtained by smearing the lens (or a filter attached to it) with petroleum jelly or by covering it with gauze or similar material. During printing, a diffusing screen is the usual means of softening the image, but the soft focus effects for which the celebrated firm of society photographers called Lenare was famous were often created during enlarging with a variety of special

lenses. All these means can create subtle and beautiful effects, but unless they ae used skilfully and sensitively can easily produce photographic clichés.

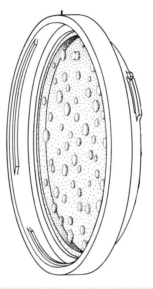

Solarization

Strictly, the complete or partial
reversal of the tones of an image as a
result of extreme overexposure. The
term is often used, however, to refer to
the SABATTIER EFFECT, which produces
results similar in appearance.

STEREO PHOTOGRAPHY

STROBE LIGHT

STURM'S MAGIC LANTERN

Stabilization
Chemical process of making superfluous SILVER HALIDES stable in prints. It is used instead of fixing and washing when rapid processing is more important than absolute print permanence.

Standard lens see page 166

Step ring
Converter that adapts a filter for use on a lens having a different thread size. A step-up, or a step-down, ring allows you to use a filter on a lens with a different thread size or diameter.

Stereo photography
Production of photographic images that give an appearance of depth approximating to that apprehended by normal human (binocular) vision. Practical stereoscopy was invented in the 1830s by the English scientist Sir CHARLES WHEATSTONE, and had a great vogue in the late 19th century. The principle involved is to produce two images taken from slightly different viewpoints through a pair of matched lenses; when the two resulting transparencies are seen through an appropriate viewer – the left-hand image by the left eye, the right-hand image by the right eye – an effect of binocular vision is produced. Projection of stereo images can be carried out by means of a beam splitter. Stereo photography has never entirely died out, but it has declined greatly in popularity since its Victorian heyday.

Stop bath
Weak acidic solution used in processing as an intermediate bath between the developer and fixer. The stop bath serves to halt the DEVELOPMENT completely, and at the same time to neutralize the ALKALINE developer, thereby preventing it lowering the acidity of the fixer. Some stop baths have indicator dyes that show when the bath is exhausted and needs replenishment.

Stop-down metering see OPEN-APERTURE METERING

Stopping down
Colloquial term for reducing the aperture of the lens.

Stress marks
Marks visible on a developed photographic image, caused by friction or pressure before processing.

Strobe light
Abbreviation for STROBOSCOPIC FLASH lamp. The term is also often used (particularly in the USA) as a colloquial term for any electronic flash unit.

Stroboscopic flash
Series of very brief flashes in rapid sequence, used to produce multiple exposure images recording progressive stages of movement. Stroboscopic flash units, which may be capable of firing thousands of times per second, are used mainly in scientific photography, but have also been used to create beautiful and revealing images of, for example, a golfer's swing.

Studio camera see LARGE-FORMAT CAMERA

Sturm, Johann see also SLR
German 17th century mathematician who may have invented the reflex system. Certainly he described in 1676 a modified CAMERA OBSCURA with a mirror angled at 45° to the lens. The image was received on oiled paper, and the camera screen covered by a hood to make easier viewing. A decade later a German monk, Johann Zahn, illustrated a camera obscura with an adjustable lens where the image was transmitted to an opal glass screen via a REFLEX mirror. Zahn also described a camera obscura fitted with a

TELEPHOTO LENS. As the Gernsheims point out in their History of Photography: 'In 1685 the camera was absolutely ready and waiting for photography.' It had to wait 150 years.

Subminiature camera
General term for cameras taking very small format film, usually of 16mm width or less. The Minox, which measures only about 18 × 30 × 80mm (96mm when it is open ready to shoot) and weighs about two ounces, is the smallest camera currently available. It has a 15mm (f5.6 fixed-focus lens giving depth of field from three feet to infinity, and takes cartridges of black and white, colour negative or colour transparency film in 8 × 11mm format. Exposure is automatically controlled, with a stepless range of shutter speeds from 1/500 to 8 seconds.

Subtractive synthesis
Means of producing a colour image by blocking (subtracting) appropriate amounts of unwanted coloured light from white light. Modern photographic processes generally use dyes or filters of three colours known as the subtractive primaries – cyan, magenta and yellow. Cyan passes blue and green but absorbs red, and is thus sometimes termed 'minus-red'; magenta passes red and blue but absorbs green (hence 'minus-green'); yellow passes red and green but absorbs blue (hence 'minus-blue). In conjunction, the three subtractive primaries are theoretically capable of producing any other colour, and if all are used together in equal amounts they will block all light and produce black. The basis of the subtractive synthesis was first systematically expounded by the French scientist Louis DUCOS DE HAURON in his book *Colours in Photography*, published in 1869, and the subtractive synthesis was gradually seen to offer more practical methods of successful colour photography than the ADDITIVE

SYNTHESIS, which had been first demonstrated in 1861.

Supplementary lens
Simple positive lens used as an accessory for close-ups. The supplementary lens fits over the standard lens, effectively reducing its FOCAL LENGTH, and permitting closer focusing.

Swing back/front
Facility found on some large-format cameras allowing the back (front) panel to be swivelled around its vertical axis. This CAMERA MOVEMENT can be used to control or distort shape or to alter the plane of focus and DEPTH OF FIELD.

Synchronization see also FLASH
Term used in photography to describe the simultaneous coupled action of flash light and SHUTTER opening.

SUBMINIATURE CAMERA
SWING BACK/FRONT

Standard lens

Lens of focal length approximately equal to the diagonal of the negative format for which it is intended, giving an ANGLE OF VIEW close to that of normal human vision. In the case of 35mm cameras, the standard lens usually has a focal length in the range 45–55mm, slightly greater than the actual diagonal of a full-frame negative (about 43mm). A standard lens for a 110 format camera has a focal length of about 24mm, for a medium-format camera about 80mm, and for a 5 × 4in camera about 200mm.

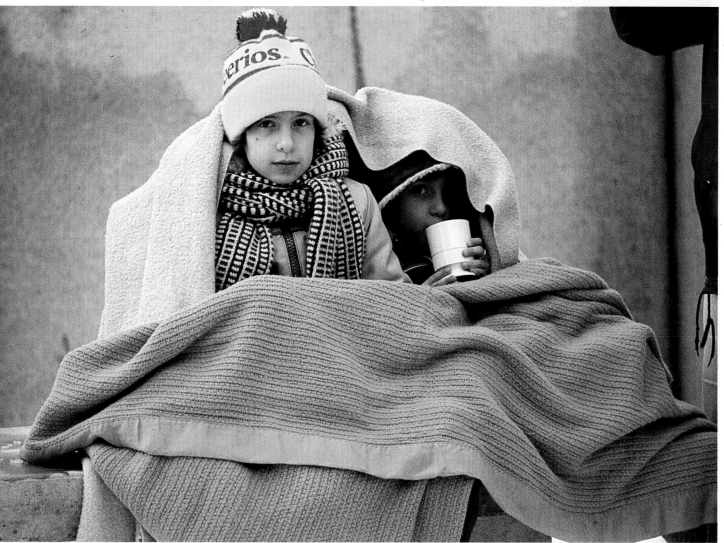

T SETTING

T setting

Shutter speed marking found on some cameras, though now mainly obsolete, and used for long (T – 'time') exposures. On veteran cameras, in particular German-made models, a Z for 'Zeit' (time) was employed instead. With the T setting you press the release once, to open the shutter, and again to close it, whereas on the more usual B SETTING the shutter remains open only as long as pressure is maintained on the release.

Tacking iron

Electrically heated device used in DRY MOUNTING to attach the bonding tissue to the print and then the print to the mount prior to permanent bonding in a press.

Technical camera see LARGE-FORMAT CAMERA

Teleconverter

Device that fits between a lens and camera body to increase the effective FOCAL LENGTH of the lens and produce a magnified image. Teleconverters come in various 'strengths', typically × 2 or × 3, and reduce the effective f number of the lens proportionally. Thus a 50mm lens set at f2 used with a × 2 converter has the effect of a 100mm lens set at f4 (a decrease of 2 stops), and the same lens used with a × 3 converter has the effect of a 150mm lens set at f5.6 (a decrease of 3 stops). Most teleconverters link with a camera's automatic DIAPHRAGM, in which case the camera's exposure meter compensates for the light loss; with non-automatic systems the necessary adjustment must be calculated and made manually. The image quality that teleconverters provide varies greatly, and is always less good than that which could be gained from a single prime lens of the equivalent focal length. Best results generally come from converters designed solely for use with specific

TELECONVERTER

TEST STRIP

lenses (Vivitar, for example, make 'Matched Multipliers' for individual lenses in their range); the performance of a converter not designed for a specific lens depends to some extent on how its optical system happens to mesh with the residual ABERRATIONS of any particular lens with which it is used. Teleconverters are generally used with lenses of focal lengths from about 50mm to 300mm; outside this range results are less likely to be of an acceptable standard.

Telephoto lens see page 170

Test strip
A simple procedure in the DARKROOM to establish the most suitable exposure for a print. Sections of a narrow strip of paper are exposed for progressively longer and longer times – usually in a doubling sequence. Strips of various papers may also be used to judge CONTRAST. Experienced printers can usually tell, by examining the negative, the grade of paper and approximate exposure time needed for an acceptable print.

Thermography
Technique of forming images by recording INFRARED radiation emitted as heat. An infrared scanner produces an image on a device similar to a television screen, different degrees of heat creating varying colours that can be recorded on conventional colour film. The shapes of the subject are usually represented on film more or less as they appear to the eye, but the colours produced are non-naturalistic, creating sometimes bizarre and beautiful effects. Thermography has various scientific applications: it can, for example, be used to record heat loss from houses, or, for medical purposes, to detect unusually hot or cold areas in the human body.

Thornton-Pickard
British firm manufacturing

high-quality SHUTTERS and cameras at the end of the 19th century. They designed roller-blind and focal plane shutters, such as the roller-blind 'Time' shutter of 1886, designed by J. E. Thornton. The firm also made a number of popular plate cameras, notably the 'Royal Ruby Reflex' and the 'Victory Reflex'.

Threshold exposure
Exposure just sufficient to produce visible density above FOG LEVEL when a sensitized material is developed.

Thyristor
Control device used in some electronic flashguns, and in particular the computer types. The purpose of a thyristor is to conserve energy by assessing the precise amount of light needed for the particular subject and distance. Because of their ability to save power instead of expending it as in the case of the more basic types of flashgun, the thyristor is able to extend battery life and give a shorter recycling time.

Tilt back/front
Facility found on some large-format cameras allowing the back (front) panel to pivot around its horizontal axis. This CAMERA MOVEMENT can be used to control or distort shape and perspective or to alter focus and depth of field.

Time/temperature development
Standard technique of processing photographic materials relying on specific developing temperature over a measured period of time to obtain the desired result.

Tintype see FERROTYPE

TLR see page 172

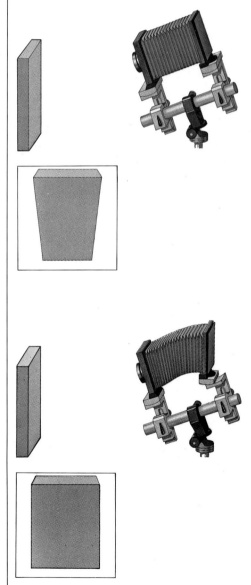

TILT BACK/FRONT

Telephoto lens

Type of LONG-FOCUS LENS having an optical construction that results in it being physically shorter than its FOCAL LENGTH. Two groups of elements, often separated by an appreciable distance, are involved – a front converging system and a rear diverging system. The rear group has the effect of lessening the convergence caused by the first group; the cone of light that reaches the image plane thus appears to converge from a point in front of the front group, producing the same effect as a lens positioned farther from the film. As most long-focus lenses are now of telephoto construction, the two terms are often incorrectly used as synonyms.

FOCAL LENGTH

FILM

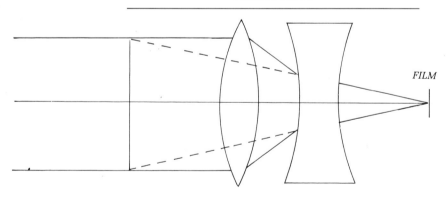

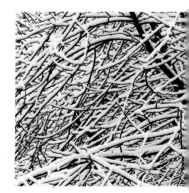

The advantages of a telephoto lens are its ability to bring distant objects in close-up, and to eliminate unwanted backgrounds on account of its shallow depth of field. Disadvantages are weight (creating camera shake, especially with slow films, or without a tripod), and limited apertures, typically f/5.6. Faster tele lenses are corresponding heavier – and expensive.

TLR

Commonly used abbreviation for the twin lens reflex camera. This type of camera has a viewing system that employs a secondary lens with a focal length equal to that of the main 'taking lens' – a fixed mirror reflects the image from the viewing lens on to a glass screen. TLR cameras suffer from PARALLAX ERROR particularly when focused at close distances, owing to the distance between the viewing lens and the taking lens. The first TLR camera was made in 1880 by R & J Beck. It took plates $3\frac{1}{4} \times 4\frac{1}{4}$in and both lenses were focused simultaneously as in the modern TLR. By far the most famous camera of this type is, of course, the Rolleiflex and still remains today the ideal precision-built twin lens reflex.

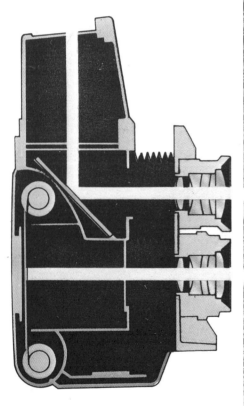

TRIPOD

Toner see page 176

Tone separation
Technique of producing a print with a limited range of distinct tonal values from a normal continuous tone negative. The technique involves making several copy negatives of different densities on lith film and printing them in register; in its most developed form it is known as POSTERIZATION.

Transparency
A photograph viewed by transmitted, rather than by reflected, light. When it is mounted in a rigid frame, a transparency is called a slide.

Tripack see INTEGRAL TRIPACK

Tripod
Camera support with three (telescopic) legs hinged together at one end to a head to which the camera is attached. Tripods are made in many sizes, from large studio models that are virtually items of furniture to miniature devices, intended mainly for table-top use, that will fit into a coat pocket. Tripods designed to be used with 35mm or medium-format cameras are most typically made of aluminium to combine durability with lightness. The feet are usually made of rubber or nylon and may be fitted with spikes for securing them firmly during outdoor use. The head to which the camera screws is generally of one of two main types: ball-and-socket and PAN-AND-TILT. In a ball-and-socket head the camera attaches to a plate mounted on a ball that can turn freely in a socket until it is locked in place, allowing the camera to be tilted or angled as desired. A pan-and-tilt head allows the same degree of movement, but it is more versatile in that it can be locked in one plane while being free to move in another at right angles to it. Most tripods have a central column so that height can be adjusted without having to move the legs. On some models the column can be reversed so the tripod can be used for low-level work, and it may also be possible to fit a lateral arm to the top or bottom of the column for added versatility. For extra stability, some tripods have braces between the central column and the legs. A recent departure from the traditional design, found in the Kennett Bembo Mk 1 tripod, is to have a central column that is continuously variable in position and not confined to the vertical plane. A useful feature found on some tripods is a device for ensuring level horizontal alignment. This may take the form of a ballbearing in a plastic compartment or a built-in spirit level.

TTL
Abbreviation for 'through-the-lens', used to characterize (1) the viewing system of single-lens reflex cameras, in which the image seen on the viewing screen is formed by light that has passed through the lens and been reflected by a mirror; or (2) camera exposure metering systems in which the light is read by the photo-electric cell(s) after passing through the lens.

Tungsten lighting see page 178

Type A colour film
Colour film balanced for tungsten lighting with a COLOUR TEMPERATURE of 3,400K. Type B colour film is balanced for tungsten lighting with a colour temperature of 3,200K. Few films are now manufactured with a type A colour balance.

U

Ultraviolet see also FLUORESCENCE
Electromagnetic radiation of WAVELENGTHS shorter than those of violet light. Ultraviolet (UV) radiation is invisible to the human eye, but most photographic materials are sensitive to it to some extent. Ordinary photographic film may show UV radiation as haze or, in the case of colour film, as a blue cast; a UV FILTER can be used to counteract these effects. UV radiation is also put to positive use in several branches of scientific photography. In photomicrography, for example, the short wavelengths of UV radiation make possible better definition of fine detail than ordinary light. Conventional glass does not have a high UV transmission, so quartz lenses are used for this work. UV radiation is highly ACTINIC (the UV content of sunlight is responsible for sunburn), so to avoid harmful effects, great care, including the use of special protective goggles, must be taken by anyone who regularly works with it.

Umbrella
Collapsible reflector made of white, or silvered, or sometimes translucent material in the form of an umbrella for use with a spotlight or flash head.

Underdevelopment
Failure to give sufficient DEVELOPMENT to a photographic material. Underdevelopment may be caused, for example, when the developing solution is exhausted, insufficiently agitated or at too low a temperature, or, more commonly, by premature removal of the material from the developer. An underdeveloped negative or transparency is thin in appearance, lacking CONTRAST and some DENSITY. An underdeveloped print is flat, pale and lifeless.

Underexposure
Failure to allow sufficient exposure either in the camera or during enlarging. Where not used deliberately for effect, it may be caused, for example, by wrongly setting the appropriate controls; incorrect judgement in difficult lighting situations; or failure to compensate for a dark filter. An underexposed negative or transparency is 'thin'; an underexposed print is flat, with little DENSITY.

Universal colour film
Colour negative film designed to be used with light of a wide range of COLOUR TEMPERATURES, variations in colour balance being made during printing.

Universal developer
Term applied to certain DEVELOPING solutions for black and white materials that are intended for use with both films and printing papers.

Up-rating see PUSHING

UMBRELLA REFLECTOR

UNDEREXPOSURE

Toner

Chemical used to impart a degree of colour to a black and white print or positive TRANSPARENCY. There are four principal types of toner, each requiring a different process for treating the print: (1) sulphide and selenium toners, which give a brownish or sepia tint to a previously bleached print by converting the (bleached) silver image to silver sulphide; (2) metallic toners, which use metal salts such as gold chloride or lead chromate to convert the silver image into metallic compounds of various colours; (3) dye toners, which deposit dye on top of the silver to colour the image; (4) colour developers, which give a dye image at the same time as the silver image.

Tungsten lighting

General term describing artificial light sources using a tungsten filament. Tungsten (sometimes called wolfram) is a heavy metallic element with a very high melting point; this property, together with its resistance to corrosion, makes it highly suitable for use in electric lamps. There are several types of tungsten lamp, the most common for photographic purposes being PHOTO FLOODS and tungsten halogen lamps. In the latter type, the glass envelope through which the filament runs contains a halogen gas (usually iodine and/or bromine). The halogen enables the lamp to maintain its colour quality throughout its life by preventing oxidized tungsten from migrating to the envelope and thereby causing blackening. Tungsten lighting is redder or 'warmer' in tone than flash or daylight, and therefore must be used with film specially balanced to match its colour temperature or with correction filters over the camera or lights. Both flash and tungsten have certain advantages and disadvantages. The main advantages of tungsten compared with flash are that it is initially cheaper to install and that it is possible to study the effects of a lighting set-up before a photograph is taken. For flash's advantages over tungsten, see FLASH.

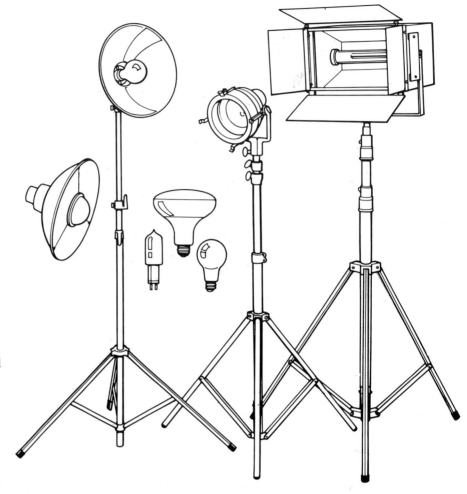

V

Viewfinder camera

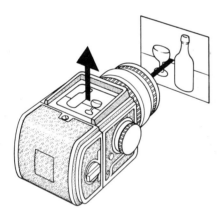

Medium format camera

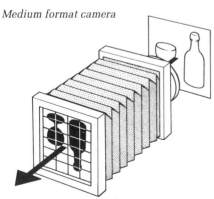

Large format camera

Variable contrast paper

Photographic printing paper sensitized in such a way as to give a variable range of CONTRAST, enabling acceptable prints to be made from a wide variety of negatives. The best-known paper of this sort is Ilford's MULTIGRADE.

Variable focus lens see ZOOM LENS

View camera see LARGE-FORMAT CAMERA

Viewfinder

'Window', screen or frame built into or attached to a camera, by means of which the photographer can see, exactly or approximately, the field of view of a lens and the area of a scene that will appear in the picture. Most viewfinders are optical (that is, they use a lens system of varying complexity) and usually incorporate a focusing mechanism and exposure information (see LCD and LED), but the simplest type of viewfinder is nothing more than a collapsible frame of wire or flat metal with a peep sight behind it. This arrangement, usually called a framefinder or sportsfinder, is often found incorporated in waist-level medium-format cameras to enable them to be used at eye-level, and is also used, for example, on old-fashioned press cameras and on many underwater cameras. Optical viewfinders are of two main types: direct vision (a framefinder is also a direct-vision viewfinder) and reflex. Direct-vision optical viewfinders use a lens system that is completely separate from the 'taking' lens of the camera, whereas in single-lens reflex cameras light passing through the taking lens is reflected by a mirror via a PENTAPRISM to the focusing screen so that viewing and taking functions are combined in the same lens. The single-lens reflex viewing system has the very great advantage over direct-vision finders that it displays, without PARALLAX ERROR, the same image that will be recorded on the film, showing the field covered by lenses of different focal lengths and taking into account the effects of filters or other lens attachments. Direct-vision viewfinders, however, have the advantages that it is easier to see the subject in dim light and that the subject is not blacked out at the moment of exposure as it is with the single-lens reflex system. (Twin-lens reflex cameras use two matched lenses one above the other – an upper viewing lens and a lower taking lens – so they have some of the advantages and disadvantages of direct-vision viewfinders.) Direct-vision optical viewfinders often incorporate lines to indicate the correction that must be made to allow for parallax, and on cameras taking interchangeable lenses they may have lines indicating the field of view for various focal lengths. These types of viewfinders are sometimes known as bright-line, suspended-frame or ALBADA VIEWFINDERS. Sophisticated SLRs may have interchangeable viewfinder heads (the Pentax LX has eight) for such purposes as waist-level viewing or angled viewing, which can be useful in flat copying. Some large-format cameras have a direct-vision viewfinder or even a coupled rangefinder, but generally the viewfinder of such cameras is the ground glass FOCUSING SCREEN.

Vignette

Picture printed in such a way that the image fades gradually into the border area. The border may be either black or white, and is produced by using a suitably shaped mask effectively to DODGE or BURN IN the whole of the central area or by FLASHING the edges of the print. Vignetting is usually employed to give a romantic, old-fashioned appearance to a picture, but it can also be used to eliminate unwanted background detail. The term vignetting is also loosely used to refer

W

to the image fall-off caused by loss of covering power, and should not be confused with cut-off caused, for example, by a too narrow lens hood.

Virtual image see REAL IMAGE

Vogel, Hermann Wilhelm

German chemist working in Berlin, and the discoverer of the fact that dyes can increase the colour sensitivity of black and white emulsions – in short, Vogel invented the orthochromatic plate. This means that an accurate rendering of tonal values is achieved, in black and white, of the colour subject, in all but the reds and orange hues. Vogel's first experiment, that of creating an isochromatic image (identical colour or tone), was made in 1873 – he is therefore the founder of orthochromatic photography, predating IVES's work of 1887, BECQUEREL's of 1875, and that of WATERHOUSE in 1876. To appreciate Vogel's unique discovery one must appreciate that the COLLODION and GELATIN DRY plates of the 19th century were unable to faithfully reproduce an approximate tonal rendering. For example, yellows and reds were always too dark, blue and violets too light because emulsions were especially sensitive to the blue end of the spectrum. Vogel's experiment was to fasten a dark blue ribbon on a piece of yellow silk, from which he made a monochromatic picture on a collodion plate. What he got was the image of a white ribbon on a piece of dark silk – in other words a reversal of the true tones. Vogel then used a yellow filter to diminish the power of the blue waves, and this gave him what he termed a 'true positive print' where the dark blue ribbon was dark, and the yellow silk was light. Vogel went on to use dyes to influence the lightwaves reaching the emulsion. He used corraline, aldehyde green, magdala red, cyanine, and fuchsine. In 1884 Vogel discovered azaline, a combination of cyanine and chinoline red, for sensitizing green, yellow and orange. Only red was wanting, and complete spectral sensitivity had to wait for pinacyanol and its discoverer BENNO HOMOLKA, in 1904.

Washing

Stage of processing that removes residual chemicals and soluble silver compounds from photographic emulsions after developing and fixing. All traces of chemicals must be thoroughly washed from negatives and prints, otherwise they will eventually attack the emulsion, causing it to decompose and spots and stains to form (see PERMANENCE). The most effective modern print washing systems spray water in from all directions at the top and siphon off chemical-laden water from the bottom.

Water softeners

Chemicals that remove or render harmless the calcium or magnesium salts present in 'hard' tap water. These impurities react with developers and may cause scum to be deposited on films. The most common water softener is washing soda (sodium carbonate), which works by precipitating the insoluble calcium or magnesium salts.

Wavelength

Characteristic determining the effects and identity of electromagnetic radiation, such as radio waves, X-rays and gamma rays. Wavelengths are measured from wavecrest to wavecrest. Different types of magnetic radiation have correspondingly different wavelengths, just as lightwaves differ to give the spectral range of colours. Waves form a cyclic sequence and the number of cycles occurring over a specific period is termed the wave's

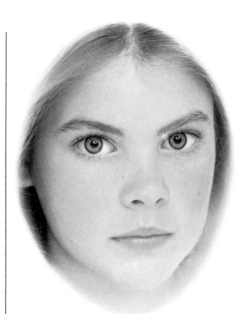

VIGNETTING

VOGEL, HERMANN WILHELM

WEDGWOOD, THOMAS

'frequency'. It is more usual to measure longwave emissions in terms of frequency, while shortwave emissions are measured in infinitesimal intervals – either in ÅNGSTROM UNITS, or in NANOMETRES – one millionth of a millimetre.

Wedgwood, Thomas

English amateur scientist, son of the potter Josiah Wedgwood, and the first experimenter – with Sir Humphry Davy – to think of exposing a light-sensitive surface in a CAMERA OBSCURA in order to record the image passing through the lens. Wedgwood's now famous experiments consisted of placing simple objects – ferns and leaves – on a surface moistened with silver nitrate. He used paper, and also white leather. He had probably arrived at leather having found that it provided a more sensitive surface, on account of the tannin, which unknown to Wedgwood acted as an accelerator (see RUSSELL, CHARLES). Davy, meanwhile, had used silver chloride in similar experiments, yet neither he nor Wedgwood were able to fix the images. Why not? Davy was a great chemist, and two possible fixing agents had already been suggested by other experimenters – common salt, for example, and ammonia. The history of photography is well endowed with speculation, and 'If only' . . . If only the scientist, Davy, had acknowledged CARL SCHEELE's discovery of ammonia as a fixing agent, or hit upon the idea of using common salt as TALBOT and DAGUERRE had done, the birth of photography might have occurred a quarter of a century earlier. 'If only' Wedgwood, who had failed to make a picture in the camera obscura, had given a much longer exposure, he might have produced the world's first photograph. But that had to wait for NIEPCE.

Wetting agent

Chemical that has the effect of lowering the surface tension of a solution, allowing it to spread evenly and quickly over a surface. Wetting agents are generally used in developers to prevent the formation of AIR BELLS, and in the final rinse to promote even drying.

Wide-angle camera see also page 184

and ANAMORPHIC LENS
Any camera that takes in a particularly wide field of view. Strictly speaking, there is a difference between a wide-angle camera, which takes a picture of normal proportions, and a panoramic camera, where the picture is wide in proportion to its height. In practice, though, the distinction is rarely made. The simplest camera of this type uses a fixed ultrawide-angle lens, and fixed, flat film: the Linhof technorama falls into this category. Such cameras produce distortion-free pictures, but are limited to fields of view of about 120° horizontally. A different approach, adopted in the Widelux camera, is to curve the film, and rotate the lens about its REAR NODAL POINT during the exposure. Using this system fields of view of up to 140° are possible. The third approach is to rotate the whole camera about the rear nodal point during exposure, and simultaneously crank the film past a narrow slit in the focal plane. This technique makes possible fields of view up to 360°, and has been used in many panoramic cameras over the years, but today notably in the Alpa Roto. Both of these latter two types of camera produce distortion: flat walls, for example, appear to bow towards the camera, and moving subjects are sometimes stretched out of all recognition.

Wide-angle lens (see p. 184–185)

Woodburytype

A very popular, successful and impressive method of photomechanical printing, in the late 19th century. It

was based on the BICHROMATED GELATIN/carbon process, and invented by an English photographer Walter Woodbury, in 1864. A GELATIN relief print was placed in contact with a lead sheet and an impression produced under hydraulic pressure. The result was an intaglio lead former, into which pigmented liquid gelatin was poured. The mould was covered by a paper backing, excess gelatin squeezed out, and left to dry. The Woodburytype, thus produced, had continuous, grain-free tone, and was indistinguishable from a photograph. It had its drawbacks, as the process of reproduction was very slow and limited to a mere half-dozen prints per former. But as a contemporary account put it, 'A Woodburytype is the finest photomechanical rendering of a photograph that anyone could wish to have.'

Working solution
Processing solution diluted to the strength at which it is intended to be used. Most chemicals are stored in a concentrated form, both to save space and to inhibit their deterioration through oxidation, but the chemical used with the Kodak Ektaflex print system, for example, is bought, used and stored at working strength.

Wratten and Wainwright
Firm of dry plate manufacturers based in Croydon, England, and the first to produce PANCHROMATIC plates using HOMOLKA's discovery Pinacyanol. The firm were pioneers of sensitometry and of colour filters, and their name endures in the catalogue of Wratten/Kodak filters in use today. So impressive were Wratten and Wainwright and their star research chemist C. Kenneth Mees (see MANNES AND GODOWSKY) that George Eastman, on a visit to Britain, poached Mees and, in order to do so, took over Wratten's, absorbing the firm into the huge Eastman Kodak corporation.

X-rays
Electromagnetic radiation in the WAVELENGTH region 0.0001–10nm. X-rays are shorter in wavelength than visible light and ULTRAVIOLET, but are longer than GAMMA RAYS. They are also known as Röntgen rays, after the German physicist Wilhelm Röntgen, who discovered them in 1895, but Röntgen himself gave them the name X-rays to indicate their unknown nature. Like light, X-rays can be reflected, diffracted or POLARIZED, and, like ultraviolet, they can produce FLUORESCENCE in certain substances; their most important property, however, is that they can penetrate solid, opaque matter. The degree of penetration depends on the DENSITY of the matter and the precise wavelengths of the rays; the shorter the wavelength, the more penetrative (or 'hard') the rays are. This property of penetration makes X-rays useful in industry and scientific research, but they are best

WIDE ANGLE CAMERA

X-RAY

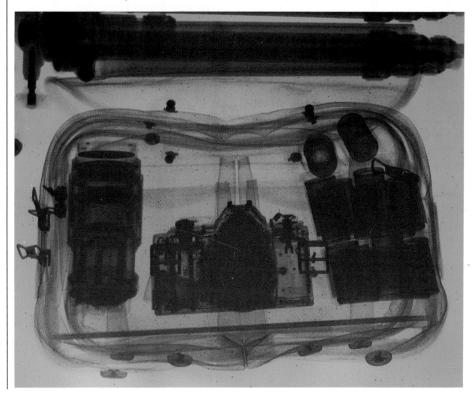

Wide-angle lens

Lens having a shorter focal length than that of a STANDARD lens for any particular format, and consequently having a wider ANGLE OF VIEW. The shorter the focal length of a lens the wider the view it will encompass. For 35mm cameras (in which the standard lens usually has a focal length of about 50mm), the most popular wide-angle lenses are of 35mm and 28mm focal length; their increased coverage is suitable for many subjects and they introduce little of the DISTORTION noticeable with more extreme wide-angle lenses. At shorter focal lengths than about 16mm, wide-angle lenses are often of FISH-EYE type and produce highly distorted images. Because of their short focal lengths, wide-angle lenses need to be placed nearer the focal plane than other lenses, and with reflex cameras this can cause a problem because they can project so far into the camera body that there is not sufficient room for the mirror to move freely. To overcome this problem, many wide-angle lenses make use of RETROFOCUS (also called inverted telephoto) construction, which means that the elements are so arranged (with a diverging front group and a converging rear group) that the BACK FOCUS is appreciably longer than the equivalent focal length.

Large-format cameras overcome the problem of short back focus by using BAG BELLOWS.

Wide-angle lenses can distort the image, especially towards the edge of the picture, but they also create dramatic and pleasing perspectives in landscapes, and with patterns of cloud against a blue sky. Try a wide-angle lens in combination with a polarizing filter.

ZEISS, CARL

X-RAY

known, of course, for their medical role in photographing the tissues and bones of the human body. The 'soft' X-rays used for this purpose are registered on special film, usually a coarse-grain emulsion coated on both sides of the film support to increase sensitivity and catch rays that pass through the first layer of emulsion. Research is currently being devoted to a method of converting conventional X-ray images into electronic information that can be stored on a computer image processor and called up for viewing on a television screen when required. X-ray films are not only bulky, but also very expensive because of their silver content, so there is a potential saving of space and money. A more important consideration, however, is that it should be possible to manipulate the electronic image so that particular parts of it can be seen more clearly, thus making diagnosis more precise. Because X-rays affect film, they can prove a hazard to photographers passing through airport security checks; the rays intended to detect weapons in baggage can fog film even through metal CASSETTES. Special lead-lined packets are available to protect film from this danger, but it is perhaps simplest and safest when passing through airports to keep all films in a separate, transparent plastic bag to be proffered for hand inspection.

Yellow

One of the three colours used in the SUBTRACTIVE SYNTHESIS. It is formed by the combination of the red and green PRIMARY COLOURS; subtracting blue from white light leaves red and green, forming yellow, so yellow is sometimes called 'minus-blue'.

Young-Helmholtz theory

Fundamental theory of colour vision first described by the English scientist Thomas Young in 1809 and subsequently confirmed by the German scientist HERMANN VON HELMHOLTZ, who rediscovered Young's work after it had lain, unread, for fifty years. It was Young who first suggested that light travels in waves and that each wavelength represented a specific colour. For example, short WAVELENGTHS are at the blue end of the SPECTRUM, long wavelengths at the red end. Young suggested that the eye interprets colours through groups of nerve fibres, each acting as a receiver for one of the primary colours, on a trichromatic principle; the retina is a receptor consisting of rod- and cone-shaped cells that interpret incoming wavelengths and build a coherent colour picture. The trichromatic principle compares to the ADDITIVE and SUBTRACTIVE SYNTHESES and, in photographic terms, to the subtractive INTEGRAL TRIPACK of modern colour film.

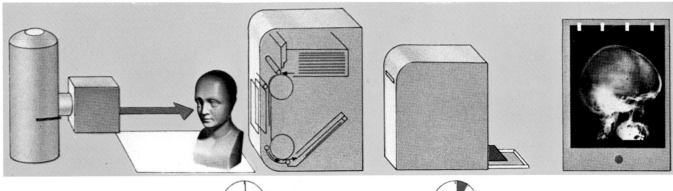

Z

Zahn, Johann see STURM

Zeiss, Carl

German optical and precision instrument manufacturer in Jena, and founded in 1846. Zeiss made some of the finest camera lenses, including the Tessar and Protar ANASTIGMATS. The Tessar, of 1902, was designed to prevent ABERRATIONS common in the symmetrical types of lens then commonly in use, employing positive and negative elements at the front, with spaces in between, and a cemented doublet of a double convex and divergent meniscus. It was a revolutionary design which other lens makers were soon to copy. Zeiss also produced a classic 35mm camera, the Contax; the Contax S of 1949 was the first camera to include a PENTAPRISM and was thus the first modern SLR.

Zoetrope

Device that produced animated movement and invented in 1833 by W. G. Horner. It was in effect a Victorian parlour entertainment, a drum pierced with slits revolving around a printed band bearing an action sequence of drawings. Spinning the drum created a sort of 'flip-book' animated progression that foreshadowed cinematography.

Zone focusing

Technique of presetting the APERTURE and focusing the camera so that the entire zone in which the subject is likely to appear is covered by DEPTH OF FIELD. This technique is particularly useful in sports or other action photography in which there is not enough time to focus the camera more accurately at the moment of shooting. The term zone focusing is also applied to the system found on some very simple viewfinder cameras in which focusing is limited to a few settings related to symbols such as a head and a range of mountains for the shortest and longest distances.

Zone system

Complex system of relating exposure readings to tonal values in picture-taking, DEVELOPMENT and printing. It was devised by Ansel Adams, and both he and another celebrated American photographer, Minor White, have written extensively on the subject.

ZOETROPE

Zoom lens

Lens in which the focal length can be continuously varied between two limits. The focal length is altered by changing the position of a group or groups of movable elements inside the lens, and in nearly all models, changes in the focal length do not affect the focus. (Lenses in which the focus has to be adjusted every time the focal length is changed should strictly be called variable focus lenses, but in practice the terms variable focus and zoom tend to be used interchangeably.) Some zoom lenses have separate control rings for focusing and zooming, while on other designs a single ring serves for both purposes (twisting the ring focuses the lens, pushing or pulling it changes the focal length). The latter type is generally known as 'one-touch'. Various ranges of focal lengths are available in zoom lenses. Most typically, they extend from wide-angle to standard (say, 28–50mm); moderate wide-angle or standard to moderate telephoto (35–70mm or 50–135mm); moderate to long telephoto (80–200mm), and wide-angle to long-focus, as in Vivitar's 28–200mm f3.5. Zooms with wider ranges are also made, however, an extreme example being Nikon's 360–1,200mm f11 zoom. Considerable improvements have recently been made by makers of zoom lenses, such as Tamron, Vivitar, Sigma and Tokina – not to mention the high-tech and expensive French Angenieux lenses. Zooms are becoming lighter and more compact as a result of the use of plastics, without sacrificing optical quality which, in some examples, can nearly equal that of a prime lens.

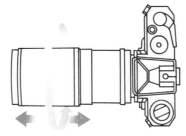

The "one-touch" zoom controls both focal length and focusing.

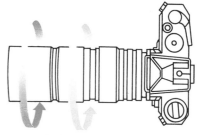

"Two-touch" lenses have separate zooming and focusing rings.

A wide-angle to long-focus zoom

*An autofocus zoom, such as Nikon's 70–210mm for the AF 501 gives sharp focus pictures through the focal range (**left**). Zooming while shooting requires practise to get the correct exposure. A night shot, such as the one **below**, needs about two seconds, while pulling back smartly on the lens barrel. Bracket several shots at different time exposures while zooming backwards and forwards.*

A zoom lens can be used
effectively to "frame" a
cluttered picture (inset). Here,
unwanted distractions, such as
the posts in the foreground
and the bridge at the top, are
masked out to focus attention
on the architectural shapes of
the boats.

Credits